in the

Western Hudson Valley

Landscape, ecology, & folklore in Orange & Ulster Counties

PEGGY TURCO

Backcountry Publications
Woodstock, Vermont

An invitation to the reader

If you find that conditions have changed along these walks, please let the author and publisher know so that corrections may be made in future printings. Address all correspondence to:

Editor, Walks and Rambles™ Series
Backcountry Publications
PO Box 748
Woodstock, VT 05091

Library of Congress Cataloging-in-Publication Data

Turco, Peggy.

Walks and rambles in the western Hudson Valley : landscape, ecology, and folklore in Orange and Ulster counties / Peggy Turco ; photographs by the author.

p.   cm.

Includes bibliographical references

ISBN 0-88150-376-2 (alk. paper)

1. Hiking—New York (State)—Orange County—Guidebooks.
2. Hiking—New York (State)—Ulster County—Guidebooks. 3. Natural history—New York (State)—Orange County—Guidebooks. 4. Natural history—New York (State)—Ulster County—Guidebooks. 5. Folklore—New York (State)—Orange County—Guidebooks. 6. Folklore—New York (State)—Ulster County—Guidebooks. 7. Orange County (N.Y.)—Guidebooks. 8. Ulster County (N.Y.)—Guidebooks. I. Title.
GV199.42.N6520737   1996

796.5'1'0974731—dc20   95-50968
                                                             CIP

Copyright © 1996 by Peggy A. Turco
10 9 8 7 6 5 4 3 2 1

Published by Backcountry Publications
A division of The Countryman Press
PO Box 748
Woodstock, VT 05091

Distributed by W.W. Norton & Company, Inc.
500 Fifth Avenue
New York, NY 10110

Printed in the Canada

Cover and text design by Sally Sherman
Maps and calligraphy by Alex Wallach, © 1996 The Countryman Press
Cover photo of the view into Ulster County Lowlands from the Northeastern Catskills, by Peter Kick
Interior photographs by the author

To the live earth of the Hudson and Delaware Valleys
and to my mother, Lucille,
who first showed me the woods.

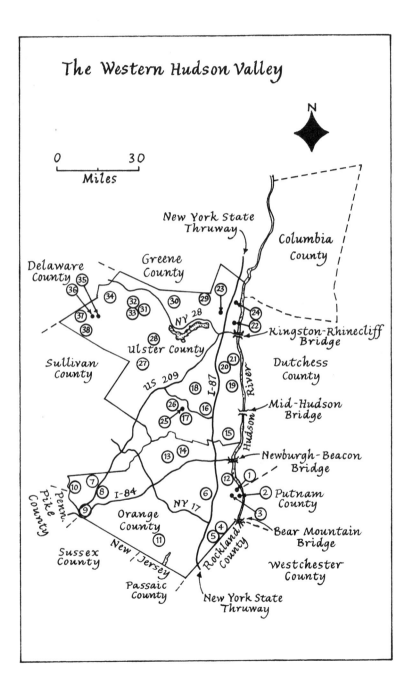

The Western Hudson Valley

N

0   30
Miles

New York State
Thruway

Columbia
County

Delaware
County   ③⑤
          ③⑥

Greene
County

          ㉓

④   ③⓪   ㉙
          ③②
      ㉝③①   ㉔
          ㉒
② ③⑦   Kingston-Rhinecliff
③⑧   NY 28   Bridge
      ㉘
      Ulster County

Sullivan   ㉗
County   Dutchess
                         County
      US 209   ⑳㉑
               ⑱   I-87   ⑲
            ㉖   Mid-Hudson
          ㉕ ⑰ ⑯   Bridge

               ⑮

      ⑬ ⑭   Newburgh-Beacon
                    Bridge

⑩ ⑦
   ⑧ I-84   ⑫   ①
⑨   ⑥   ② Putnam
   Penn.   County
   Pike Orange   ③
   County County   Bear Mountain
         ⑪   ④   Bridge
                  ⑤
Sussex   Rockland
County New Jersey County Westchester
                           County
Passaic
County   New York State
            Thruway

Hudson River

Contents

Acknowledgments

Special thanks to Vickie Doyle, Jonathan Garen, Peter Osborne, and Stephen Scherry.

Thanks also to Scott Anderson, Michael Bacher, Tom Backus, Spider Barbour, Ellyce Cavanaugh, Jack Focht, John Gebhards, Ann Gilchrist, Anne Guenther, Timothy Harley, Carl Helstrom, Huguenot Historical Society, Ken Kittle, Klyne Esopus Historical Society, Reba Laks, Bob Larsen, Randy and Karen Martis, John Meyer, Ruth Anne Muller, Peg Olsen, Joe Pesch, Mickey Petrillo, Charles Platt, George Profous, George Schuler, Norman Shapiro, Graham Skea, Tim Sullivan, Daniel Terpening, Pat Viscering, Ray Wood, and Neil Zimmerman.

Introduction

On a clear summer's day I climbed Sky Top stone tower at Mohonk Mountain House in the Shawangunks to take a look at the territory for this book. I had seen the view many times before, but now I had a project in mind. Swallows winnowed the breeze as I surveyed much of the land I must walk: half the Hudson Highlands, all the northern Shawangunk, half the Catskill Mountains, and the river valleys and hills in between. It is huge, I thought.

I spent two years walking to collect the descriptions in this book. I grew up in the Hudson Valley, so I was already familiar with many of the sites I revisited. Yet, my home region never ceases to provide new mountains, woods, rivers, cities, history, and people for me to discover. This vastness and diversity amazes me. The mental map of my "home" has grown into something the size of the state of Massachusetts.

The land has so much to say. I have chosen to focus here on the different counties of Orange and Ulster to provide the reader and rambler with a greater diversity of ecological and historical descriptions. This quarters the Hudson Highlands and halves the Catskills along arbitrary political borders; however, it keeps much of the Shawangunk Ridge intact. Furthermore, the lowland ridges and valleys of the two counties—particularly the Wallkill, Rondout, Esopus, and Neversink Valleys—share a common historical heritage. My hope is that the reader will use this guide to better understand the natural communities and human-use history of the region. Each chapter covers some aspect of the Hudson or Delaware Valley ecosystem. Put them together and you gain a whole picture of a living landscape.

The chapters are divided into upland and lowland sections grouped according to their geology. Bedrock and climate predetermine the type of soil, flora, fauna, and human use that occurs at a site. The eldest come first: that's the Hudson Highlands, mostly formed during the Precambrian period 1200 million years ago. Then comes

A tiger swallowtail butterfly feeds on tall meadow rue (Thalyctrum pubescens), *a plant of moist soils that in July is topped by a foamy star-burst of white flowers.*

Schunemunk, with a section all its own. The Shawangunks follow next, a mere 435 million years old. The lowland ridge and valley province in between these ranges is slightly older at 500 million years of age. The Appalachian plateau of the Delaware Valley chapters and the Catskills are the most recent, both formed 395 million years ago. All of these places were created before the evolution of mammals. The Hudson Highlands were as tall as today's Rocky Mountains when no animals lived on the planet except invertebrates.

These nature walks guide you on trails where you are legally allowed to park your car and walk. For many sites, each chapter is only a taste of what the park acreage has to offer. Some walks are very short. Others are full-day hikes that climb mountains. One travels within a city. The plant and animal descriptions offer information on dominant species found living within the park. If you do not find one of the plant species noted in a chapter, keep an eye out for it elsewhere; sooner or later you will come across it in your travels. Expect to find it where conditions match those described in the chapter. "Expect," however, may be too strong a word. It seems anytime you establish a "rule" in ecosystems, exceptions to that rule abound. Natural communities are still far too complex and unpredictable for the dismissal of human description.

I have included the Latin along with the common names of most of the plants so that you can continue your studies in other field guides. The scope of this book does not allow for all I would like to say about the multitude of fascinating medicinal and edible virtues of the plants, nor their ecology, habits, form, or history. The same can be said for animal species and human-use history. Use this guide as an introduction that can lead you on a path of discovery.

Human use of the region extends back in time for at least 8000 years, making this ancient land. Many place-names are Lenape words: Neversink, Shawangunk, Mohonk, Schunemunk, and Esopus are just a few. The Lenape, or Delaware, people are classified into two basic linguistic groups: Unami and Munsee. Munsee was spoken on both banks of the lower and mid-Hudson and upper Delaware River Valleys, while Unami was spoken south of the Raritan River and the Delaware Water Gap. Corruption of the original Lenape by 3 centuries of various non-Native speakers has garbled some of the words, yet others are preserved nearly intact. Throughout the text I have attempted to explain, where possible, the meaning of Native place names. I try to avoid historic interpretations that failed to consult speakers of the language. My childhood teacher, He Who Stands Firm/Nicholas Shoumatoff, provided the information on speakers' interpretations. Also consulted were William Beauchamp's *Aboriginal Place Names of New York* and Edward Ruttenber's *Footprints of the Red Men: Indian Geographical Names.* The various Indian words used in Harriman State Park are largely nonindigenous, whimsically chosen from Beauchamp's collection of Iroquois, Lenape, Mahikan, and other New York State place-names when the park was first developed.

Six chapters lead you to parks along the full lengths of two major rivers—the Esopus and the Neversink—once at their births, again in their middles where fully formed, and once more at their mouths. In this manner you gain a feel for the rivers as complete, living entities. The Wallkill, the Mongaup, and the Delaware are

The shining, white quartz conglomerate of the Shawangunks supports one of the world's rare habitats.

other major rivers visited in various parks, along with several minor tributaries. What makes the region unique, though, is the estuary of the Hudson River. The Hudson Valley trough itself funnels migrating birds along the eastern edge of the continent. On and in the river, tides, ships, sea gulls, and a mediated local climate lend a touch of the ocean. The varying salt front brings waves of blue-claw crabs and spawning sea fishes and, now and then, a whale. At all times of year the deep center channel harbors the giant sturgeon. Chapters describe three shoreside parks in Ulster and a black sand beach and three mountain peaks in Orange that showcase the Hudson River.

Ways of Woodsfolk

Please take good care of our parks. Do not litter. Do not trample vegetation off the trail. The considerate woodsman does not smoke on the trail and never leaves butts, cans, gum wrappers, or anything else but footprints. Plants are never collected, picked, or injured. Animals are left undisturbed. The quiet walker sees the most wildlife.

For the beginning hiker it is easy to be miserable in the woods.

The bugs are biting, the poison ivy is thriving, Lyme disease threatens, it is too cold, it is too hot, you are tired; the list of discomforts can be endless. Biting bugs are nasty, it's true, but don't allow them to overwhelm you. Ignore them. Take them in stride. Discomfort is more a concept of the mind. Dwell on mosquitoes and you will be eaten alive, never again to set foot on a trail. Dwell on the beauty of the trees and the spacious, open air and, no matter how much they bite, you will barely notice the bugs. The more you dwell on a negative thing, the larger it grows. Do not let discomforts ruin your rambles. Do not let fear keep you from the woods.

The prepared hiker carries a light pack with food, water, a trail map, compass, and extra clothes. Rain gear is carried if the weather is questionable. Sturdy hiking shoes or boots are worn. Remember that the high peaks of the Catskills can experience wintry weather in October and May. But even a sudden thunderstorm on a sultry July afternoon can chill with hail, rain, and wind.

For each park, I note the route distance and comment on the approximate walking time for longer hikes. This is my own walking time, which allows for plenty of exploring and stops for scenic admiration. A fast hiker can clip through in less time.

Know the trail marking code:

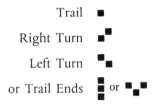

Trail maintenance people stack small logs or branches across trails to indicate that the paths are closed or undesirable. Respect posted property signs. The legend below gives the symbols used on the maps:

parking   Ⓟ
main trail   ● ● ●
side trail or alternate route   · · · · ·

bridge	⤣
stone wall	⬿⬿
pond/lake	⬯⬮
view	☼
paved road	▬
dirt road	⸺
stream	⬳
summit	△
vegetation boundary	⌇⌇⌇
ledges	⟩⟩⟩
barrier gate	⁄
mine	✕
bushwhack	○ ○ ○
swamp	⤓
building	■
foundation/ruin	⊏⊐

The Hudson Highlands

The Hudson River twists and flows at its deepest and narrowest through the Appalachian cordillera of the Hudson Highlands. The view here is north from The Timp in Bear Mountain State Park.

The Hudson Highlands

This is the oldest land described in this book. The granite and gneiss of ancient Appalachians—the eroded nubs of once great mountains—were breached by the glaciated Hudson River fjord. Few people have ever wanted to live here. The stony hills are difficult to farm, hunt, or inhabit. Esopus, Wappinger, Mahikan, Dutch, Huguenot, English, and other peoples mostly looked up at the hills from their boats on their way north or south to gentler, more productive, bottomland soils.

Yet, of course, all of these peoples did use the Highlands, rich in upland game animals, timber, rocks, metals, and solitude. Europeans turned the tangible resources into commodities. The entire range was clear-cut mostly for sawmills and charring into charcoal. Only a tree here or there was left to shade free-ranging cattle and swine, animals that compacted the drying soil and competed with native species. The hills were quarried for stone and mined for iron. This sort of wholesale exploitation and destruction not only in the Highlands but especially in the Palisades just downriver prompted the outcry for preservation that helped change America and the world. The views you see from these mountains helped mold the sublime age that believed a view had intrinsic, aesthetic worth that outweighed financial gain through consumption. That spark went on to inspire the national park system, which in turn became the model for national parks around the world.

These hills and river have been a catalyst for other national conservation events. In 1927 the American Museum of Natural History opened Trailside Museums at Bear Mountain, the world's first outdoor museum, to help New York City visitors appreciate the natural world within natural surroundings, in the birth of environmental education. Scenic Hudson's battle to save Storm King from Consolidated Edison, which wanted to build a power plant, started the national environmental movement that spawned the 1969 National Environmental Policy Act and New York's State Environmental Quality Review Act. Clearwater's battle to save the Hudson River initiated America's search for clean water.

Storm King

Location: Cornwall/Highlands
Distance: 2 miles
Owner: State of New York

Sometimes frightened Dutch skippers and crew within the clutches of the Wind Gate on the Hudson River looked up at the cliff brow of this forbidding mountain and there saw local spirits unleashing thunderstorms to sink them. At other times hungry Dutch folk saw a well-rounded shape that reminded them of a big pat of butter: thus, the old names Klinkenberg and Boterberg (Sounds Hill and Butter Hill). The romantic poet Nathaniel Parker Willis lobbied successfully to change the name to Storm King, to his mind a more noble label.

Some easy rock scrambling brings you to one of the Hudson Valley's most storyful hills. Visit any time of year (although the panorama is most extensive when the leaves are down) for what probably ranks as the finest view of Newburgh Bay and the Long Reach.

Access

Parking is provided at a scenic highway rest stop where US 9W reaches its highest point on the pass over Storm King at the head of Mother Cronk's Clove (said to be the exact spot where the pixies brewed their storms). However, since this is a divided highway, the rest stop is accessible only from the northbound lane. The lot lies 1.6 miles south from the Angola Road overpass in Cornwall, and 3 miles north of the NY 218 overpass at West Point.

Trail

The yellow-marked trail begins at the north end of the parking lot beside the highway and climbs along the road cut into a red and scrub oak and hickory habitat over outcrops of Hudson Highlands granite striped in black bands of gneiss. Right away you gain views, but I will wait until the summit of Butter Hill—the round knob that looms

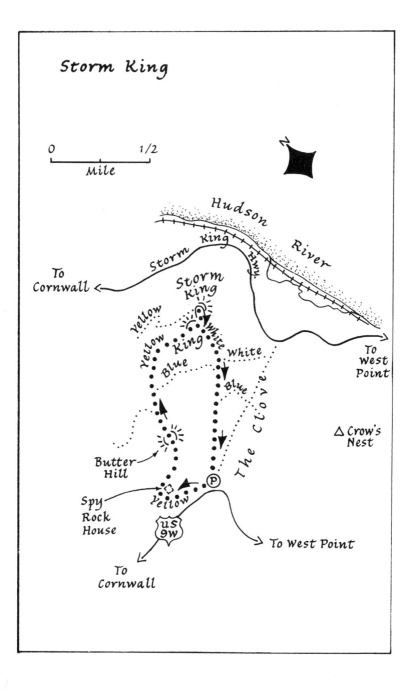

ahead—to describe them. Pass the ruins of a building whose foundation is constructed of local granite. This was Spy Rock House, the cottage of New York City physician Edward Lasell Partridge, a chief proponent in the crusade to save the Hudson Highlands. Descend a small ravine. In mid-April watch for Dutchman's breeches *(Dicentra cucullaria)*, a small woodland plant with lacy foliage and white and yellow flowers that look like, well, a Dutchman's breeches—you know, those flared pantaloons.

Climb through talus of the moist ravine slope past black birch, red maple, and moosewood and up steep Butter Hill. Perhaps this symmetrical round knob was Boterberg, and the imposing rocky summit overlooking the Wind Gate was Klinkenberg. Just a theory of mine; Europeans in their homeland like to name every feature. At the dry crest find stunted scrub oak, paper birch, pitch pine, blueberry, huckleberry, sweet fern, grasses, and mosses. These are fire-resistant plants adapted to survival on the dry mountain crests of the Hudson Highlands, which are naturally subject to brush fires.

Keep on until the United States Geodetic Survey benchmark pins your location on the summit of Butter Hill. When the leaves are down, you have a 360-degree view. Looking back the way you came rise the fire tower and hills of Black Rock Forest. See the few conifers on the north slope crest of Black Rock (the part of the hilltop people would see from the valley floor) that gave the hill its name? To the north of that lies supine Schunemunk, creased by the hemlock ravines of Deep Hollow and Baby Brook. The Orange County floor runs westward to the Wurtsboro Ridge of the southern Shawangunk spine. Follow that ridge to its highest elevation at Sam's Point and on along all the northern Shawangunk. Behind that loom the Catskills. In the foreground is the village of Cornwall, the Newburgh-Beacon Bridge, Newburgh Bay, and the river past Danskammer Point up the Long Reach to Poughkeepsie, the Marlboro Hills, and Shaupeneak. On the Hudson's east bank spreads Dutchess County north to Stissing Mountain. North and South Beacon Mountains and Scofield Ridge lift up from the valley floor. Behind them rise the hills of Sharpe Reservation and the Fishkill Range reaching to near the Connecticut border, and the southern Taconics. Immediately east of you is the summit of Storm King. On the other side of the Hudson rises Bull Hill, marred by the quarry scar; Little Stony Point; Cold Spring; the communications tower on the Fahnestock plateau; and the hills of Putnam and a bit of Westchester Counties. Directly across from Butter Hill is Crow's Nest. The deep valley between the two is The Clove, also known as Mother Cronk's Clove. In sailing days the wind that gathers and speeds down this valley into the Hudson River was infamous for its destructive power and the sinking of ships.

Follow downhill slightly and along the ridge. At the intersection with the blue-marked Howell Trail, keep left on the yellow trail. A gradual climb brings you to a view from the north edge of Storm King, a river panorama of Newburgh Bay and its surrounding hills. At Storm King's summit, just over 1300 feet, grows a small field of black chokeberry *(Aronia melanocarpa,* formerly *Pyrus),* spurge (*Euphorbia* sp.), and grasses. Within rock crevices bloom thick bouquets of early saxifrage *(Saxifraga virginiensis)* and rock sandwort *(Minuartia michauxii,* formerly *Arenaria stricta)* in late April. Continue downhill eastward on the yellow trail past many herd paths (this is a popular spot). Watch the bedrock outcrop on your right, smothered in April by early saxifrage mixed with a little mountain sandwort *(Minuartia groenlandica),* the tundra cousin of the rock sandwort. The yellow trail bends left to another view south and east. The trail continues, but this is the last stop before you begin the return route.

Far below where you cannot see it, the Storm King Highway, a feat of engineering in its day, was hewn into the granite by African American laborers who took their lives into their hands dangling off the edge of the sheer drop. Also invisible at the northeastern foot of Storm King, a shaft plumbs 1114 feet below sea level and from there beneath the Hudson River across to Breakneck and underneath Bull Hill. This is the 14-foot-diameter tube of the Catskill Aqueduct, which brings Catskill mountain water from Ashokan Reservoir to the faucets of New York City at the rate of 500 million gallons a day. They had to sink the shaft that deep to reach bedrock. As high as Storm King rises, the Hudson River gorge plumbs deeper, yet it is buried beneath the debris of glaciation: layers of sand, silt, clay, and gravel.

The view from Storm King south to the Hudson River's east bank includes Little Stony Point, the village of Cold Spring, and Constitution Island. On the west bank to the right rises the north ridge of Crow's Nest.

You might see dancing butterflies while you visit any of these mountaintops. When ready to mate, many species seek out hilltops as their meeting places. Black swallowtail and Edwards hairstreak are common butterflies on dry Hudson Highland summits. Return uphill on the yellow trail. Just before the saxifrage outcrop and before the view northward, watch for a somewhat obscure left turn onto the white-marked trail. Follow along the ridge line, then plunge into The Clove and along the slope at a height. This will lead you to the blue trail. Turn left to continue along The Clove wall, descending slightly. Where the blue trail turns sharply left down into The Clove, keep straight on an unmarked trail, actually an old road, through the tall woodland in the shadow of Butter Hill. The end of this lovely woodland walk leads up the ugly fill for US 9W and the parking lot.

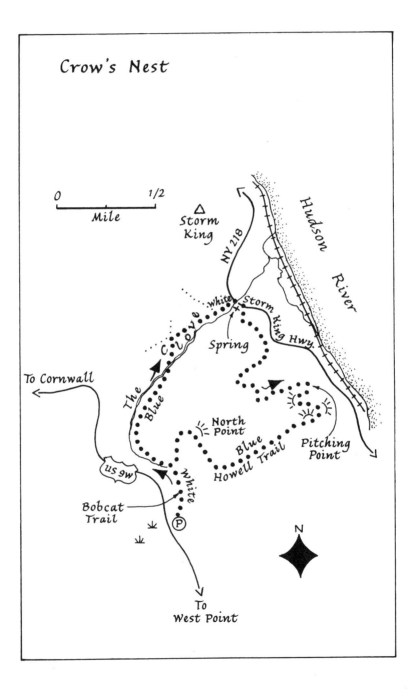

Crow's Nest

0   1/2
Mile

△ Storm King

NY 218

Hudson River

white

The C l o v e

Storm King Hwy.

Spring

To Cornwall

Blue

North Point

Blue Howell Trail

Pitching Point

US 9W

white

Bobcat Trail

ⓅP

N

To West Point

Crow's Nest

Location: West Point
Distance: 8 miles
Owner: State of New York

Crow's Nest is a mountain with a bowl-shaped summit, the subject of a Victorian poem famous in its day. It was one of the favorite haunts of turn-of-the-century photographer and writer William Thompson Howell. During the Civil War, Crow's Nest made a great target for testing Parrot guns manufactured at the West Point Foundry at Cold Spring. Today half the mountain is owned by the military academy at West Point, which keeps its property off limits to the public.

A short and easy walk with a view takes you out to the first bluff with a backtrack for a return. Or you can continue to the north peak of Crow's Nest and again return the same way. Or, you can go all the way along the new Howell Trail to one of the historic pitching points, down to Old Storm King Highway, and loop home through The Clove.

Access

From the intersection of US 9W, NY 293, and NY 218 just west of West Point, head north on US 9W, climbing for 2.6 miles to a parking pull-off on your right as you start going downhill. Slow down as you approach; it is a sharp pull-off onto dirt and gravel. There is no access from the southbound lane of US 9W. The trail was created and is maintained by the New York–New Jersey Trail Conference.

Trail

Begin on the white-marked Bobcat Trail. You are already high up on the crest of Crow's Nest in a spare, xeric forest of red and chestnut oak, mountain laurel, and heaths. Bobcat Trail runs into the Howell

Trail at the head of Mother Cronk's Clove, also known as The Clove, the low-slung valley that lies between Storm King and Crow's Nest. The Cronks were a family who settled in this valley in the 1800s. Watch carefully for the right turn onto the blue-marked Howell Trail, which leads up-slope. If you find yourself going steeply downhill, you have passed the turnoff and are on the return route.

A short, moderately steep climb that flushes towhee and extended-family groups of robins from the blueberries and huckleberries brings you to a view through the stunted chestnut oaks across The Clove to the monolith of Butter Hill. Walk the crest working your way upward. A grassy knoll just past a large erratic—a boulder dropped here by a glacier—provides the first view across the Hudson River of Bull Hill and Breakneck Ridge. The rim of Crow's Nest's bowl—where you are headed—slopes to your right.

The path next traverses Crow's Nest's long flank winding upward and along. Nearing the river you arrive at another grassy knoll, with fabulous views of Pollepel Island within the North Gate, Storm King with the highway cut into it, and Little Sugarloaf. The vegetation is a bewildering combination of moosewood and pitch pine *(Pinus rigida)* and an open area being colonized by a dense growth of gray birch saplings. The Hudson Highlands represent the Hudson Valley's southern range limit of moosewood, also known as striped maple. It is common in the Catskills, where it is an important component in woods of moist soils. Pitch pine appears in sparse amounts on some of the extreme parched crests of the Highlands (Popolopen Torne is the only mountain other than Crow's Nest with a large population). In the Shawangunk, pitch pine makes up entire pine barrens. The wide variation in soil depth on Highland slopes, from exposed bedrock to pockets of deep soil trapped between rocks, leads to a wide variation in soil moisture and the strange mix of plant species. Also, large populations of both moosewood and hemlock inhabit the north-facing slope of The Clove. The Hudson Highlands, the Hudson Valley, and even New York State as a whole are located at the range limit of many northern, southern, upland, and lowland plant species. These species occurring at the ends of their ranges tend to mix in combinations unknown elsewhere.

Keep on to the bedrock outcrop for an outstanding view of Newburgh Bay, Little Sugarloaf, Breakneck Ridge, Scofield Ridge, North and South Beacon Mountains, and Bull Hill, with its quarry scar. At your feet is Little Stony Point (its impressive cliff face was blasted away by quarrymen in the 1800s). On hot summer weekends the cove there is crowded with anchored boats and bathers basking on Sandy Beach. Continuing southward roll the hills of Putnam County, the village of Cold Spring, Foundry Brook Cove, Constitution Marsh, Constitution Island, and the World's End bend in the Hudson River.

If you want to see Pitching Point and go for the entire loop, the trail leads steeply down the north face of the mountain, where you get to see another incongruity: hemlock and pitch pine together. Another wonderful view is seen here of Storm King, Butter Hill, and the U-shaped Clove, with its grand sweep of forest canopy. The hemlocks here are flagged to the east-southeast.

Howell Trail leads down stone stairs and a steep slope. Pitching Point is a natural cliff chute of stone where in the mid-1800s timberers shot whole logs into the Hudson River for loading and shipment, a sight gawked at by steamship passengers.

The trail now leads steeply down through a hemlock forest dying from wooly adelgid infestation. The Highlands seem to be near the limit of this blight that is eliminating the hemlock as a forest component. At first it was feared the wooly adelgid would suck the life out of hemlocks from the Hudson to the Mississippi and beyond, but perhaps the genetic makeup of the hemlock changes sufficiently with distance from New York City, or perhaps a difference in climate precludes adelgid survival. Whatever the reason, in the Catskills you do not see what you find in Mother Cronk's Clove.

The Clove was known for its lovely, dark hemlocks. The trail switchbacks down to meet dead and dying conifers. The valley is still forested. Compare the massive and towering red oaks of this valley with the stunted ones you saw up on top of the summit. Genetically, they are the same species and are probably the same age, too. "Clove" comes from the Dutch *kloof,* which means "ravine."

Howell Trail leads to a memorial to the Stillman Spring. Go to Storm King Highway, cross the brook, and pick up the white-marked

The north ridge of Crow's Nest (left) and Storm King
as seen from Cold Spring

trail that leads up The Clove. This meets an old road and then intersects the blue trail. Keep straight on the old roadbed, now the blue trail. The easy-to-moderate climb brings you back into the dry soil of heaths and laurel. Unfortunately, as you climb straight up The Clove, traffic on busy US 9W destroys any sense of wilderness. The trail steepens as you gain the head of The Clove and meet the white trail where you first began the loop. Follow the white Bobcat Trail back to your car.

Black Rock Forest

Location: Cornwall and Highlands
Distance: 5 miles
Owner: Black Rock Forest Preserve and Consortium

The 3600-acre, privately owned forest stands out from afar as a dozen rounded mountain heads clustered atop the northwestern edge of the Hudson Highlands plateau, one hill surmounted by a fire tower. All these bumps are smaller than the adjacent and formidable Storm King.

Previously owned by Harvard University for 40 years, Black Rock Forest was purchased in 1989 by a consortium of institutions that use the land for scientific research and education, including the American Museum of Natural History, Brookhaven National Laboratory, Brooklyn Botanic Garden, and 12 universities, colleges, and schools. In this diverse place of deciduous woodland, conifers, lakes, brooks, fields, and marshes, the rambler could easily wander for days. However, the consortium asks that the public restrict itself to the more popular roads so that remote, fragile habitats and study areas remain undisturbed.

This walk takes you to Black Rock, where there is a spectacular view of the Hudson Valley. This is probably the preserve's most popular public destination; however, do not expect much company during your visit. Black Rock Forest is practically unknown except to local residents, and it is a huge place. After this introduction, you can explore other routes.

Access

From the Angola Road overpass intersection of US 9W and Angola Road just outside the village of Cornwall-on-Hudson, proceed south on US 9W. In 0.5 mile you will pass the preserve's offices located on

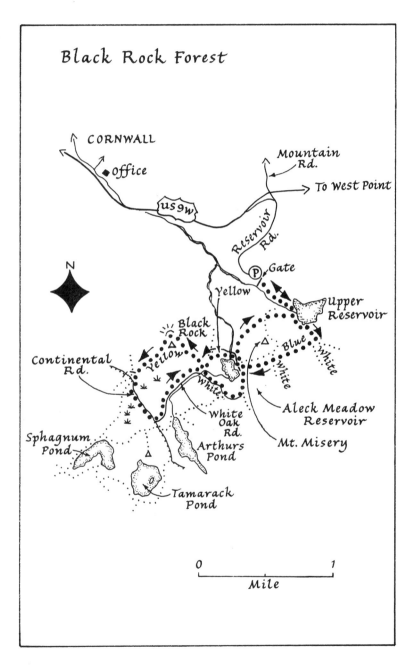

your left along a parallel side road in a white house—stop in for a map. Do not wander around this preserve without a map. At bookstores you can purchase the New York–New Jersey Trail Conference map 7 for west Hudson Trails. Continue on US 9W for another 0.8 mile, climbing the Hudson Highland escarpment, and turn right at a small sign for Black Rock Forest. This spur road has no name and will take you into Black Rock Hollow for 0.3 mile to a house and a small soccer field. Just past these, at the T-intersection turn right onto Reservoir Road. Shortly, the road turns to dirt. Proceed along the exciting, precipitous rim of the hollow for 0.7 mile to a parking lot on your left.

If you are approaching from the south on US 9W, just after the summit of Storm King slow down as you descend to turn a hard right onto Mountain Road, looping beneath US 9W by way of a one-lane tunnel. At the T-intersection, keep straight onto Reservoir Road.

The preserve is open dawn to dusk all year, but closed during times of fire danger and during deer-hunting season. Dogs are allowed on leash only. Mountain biking is prohibited except by members of the Black Rock Mountain Bike Club (call 914-534-2966 for membership information). For more information about Black Rock Forest, call the preserve manager and director at 914-534-4517.

Trail

From the parking lot, walk around the gate and down the gravel road. This is the old route that connected West Point to Cornwall before US 9W or Storm King Highway existed, used by stagecoaches and militia. The preserve is crisscrossed by many old Continental army roads, mining paths, farm lanes, and logging roads. The area was well used before it became a preserve. The road gently angles up a large earthen dam to the first lake of your visit, called Upper Reservoir. Black Rock Forest contains many artificial lakes, part of the water supply for Cornwall and Highland Falls. Swimming, boating, and fishing are forbidden.

From the dam keep straight around the lake shore. At the fork, bear right away from the lake. Watch for a right turn onto the blue-marked trail, an old farm road lined with stone walls. Shortly, this runs into the white-marked trail. Turn right to keep on the blue trail. Follow through an open and lovely woodland carpeted with sedges, past many stone walls from the farming past in which chipmunks live. Keep straight through the intersection with the next white trail.

At the dirt road, turn right and shortly left at the gate for Aleck Meadow Reservoir. Go downhill alongside the spillway where the yellow-marked trail crosses the stream on a bridge and the water plunges into a dark hemlock forest. Keep across the foot of the dam, and at the intersection with the white trail turn left, keeping on the yellow trail. When you see the road, follow the yellow trail as it bends right to begin the climb up Black Rock.

The higher you climb, the drier, more xeric the soil conditions become and the shorter the oaks grow. At the summit (1410 feet), find red and bear or scrub oak, black cherry, some pitch pine, and the heaths. Emerge out of the closed-in woods to an enormous and sudden view that will take your breath away. Starting at the far left from the closed fire tower, you can see Sphagnum Pond if the leaves are down and then the hills of Black Rock Forest. Behind them lies Schunemunk, with the towers on its southern ridge crest. At the foot of the Hudson Highlands escarpment lies the pond at Kenridge Farm of the Museum of the Hudson Highlands. Then northward spreads the Orange and Ulster County floor, with the entire span of the Shawangunk on the horizon from Wurtsboro Ridge to Rosendale, and all the Catskills, the Marlboro Hills, and Shaupeneak. Then eastward across Newburgh Bay is the Hudson River to Dutchess County, in whose northern reaches can be seen Stissing Mountain and the south Taconics. And still eastward are the Beacon Mountains, Breakneck Ridge, Storm King, and Butter Hill, with its cliff.

In the cracks of the bedrock grows dwarf cherry *(Prunus pumila* var. *susquehanae),* no higher than an herb. The (very) few pitch pine, hemlock, white pine, and red cedar of Black Rock's summit serve just enough to darken this hill, a contrast to the nearby deciduous hilltops when viewed from the valley floor far below. This summit became a landmark to lowland farmers, and thus it gained its name. The "rock" is the mountain itself, and the "blackness" comes from the conifers. William Thompson Howell wrote in 1906: "Old man Green once

Pitch pine (Pinus rigida) *at the summit of Black Rock Forest*

told me that the slopes of Black Rock were once largely clothed with white pine, and that he as a young man lumbered there." It seems Black Rock used to be blacker.

Painted blue footprints lead across the bedrock to a stone with a view of the Hudson River, Storm King, Whitehorse Mountain, and Bull Hill. Return to the summit and follow the yellow trail, which descends the rock face in the direction of the closed fire tower. Specimen trees along the way have been labeled. Here is a chance to learn the different oaks. At the dirt road, keep left on the yellow trail. Shortly you arrive at the intersection with another dirt road. If you would like a longer walk (2 extra miles) around deep Sphagnum and Tamarack Ponds, then keep straight ahead into the red pines on the dirt road.

If you are not visiting those ponds, then turn left onto Continental Road following the nature trail signs. This is the old military trail tramped by thousands of Revolutionary War Continentals on their way to the last cantonment at New Windsor. At the giant white oak turn left onto White Oak Road, still following the nature trail. The road leads downhill parallel to the brook heading downstream.

Pass the beginning of the yellow trail's ascent of Black Rock. Continue along the road downhill and around Aleck Meadow Reservoir. At the next intersection with a road, keep left to complete the circle around Aleck Meadow Reservoir. Keep straight past all intersections into dark hemlocks. Watch on your right for a small wet area where a culvert runs beneath the road. Here, in May, marsh marigold blooms among tall violets. This is a wetland species; it is unusual to be able to view marsh marigold so closely and still keep your feet dry.

The road skirts Mount Misery. Watch the right verge for trailing arbutus. This road leads all the way to Upper Reservoir. Keep left down the dam and straight on to your car.

Harriman State Park

Plants that inhabit acidic, perched bogs such as Pine Swamp are adapted to growing in nutrient-poor conditions.

Harriman State Park

Harriman (46,647 acres) and adjacent Bear Mountain (5067 acres) State Parks evoke superlatives. This huge tract of Hudson Highlands, contiguous with the wilds of Sterling Forest and the New Jersey Highlands state properties, creates an enormous reservoir of flora and fauna. There are resident populations of black bear and timber rattlesnake scant miles from New York City. Hikers can easily lose themselves here for weeks of exploration. Both the Appalachian Trail and the Long Path pass along these hills. In fact, the very first section of the Appalachian Trail to be built was at Bear Mountain. Facilities include 200 public campsites, 35 organization camps, 40 public cabins, 11 shelter lean-tos, 200 miles of marked trails, uncounted more miles of unmarked trails, three swimming beaches, 175 acres of picnic areas, 19 family cemeteries, numberless ruins and foundations, 18 furnace or mine sites, and 15 rock shelters, to list just a few. And yet on a recent July 4th weekend the park had to close, saturated with visitors. This is one of New York City's playgrounds, yet a paltry few visit the vast acreage of backcountry. It is an excellent park to walk in autumn, because hunting is always forbidden.

The land has been timbered, mined, and farmed. Revolutionary War battles have been fought in these valleys, and whole towns have come and gone. Two chapters cannot do even a hair's breadth of justice to the richness of this park. Worse yet, the parameters of this book cut the park right in half along an arbitrary political line. Thus The Timp, Dunderberg, Doodletown, and all the other fabulous and famous sites of southern Harriman are not in this collection. But no matter. There is enough over the Orange County line to deal with, and that but a sampling. Return to Harriman time and again; you'll never grow tired of the place.

Demand on the acreage is so great and the staff and budget so small that regulation of visitors is a real concern. You cannot park at a trailhead unless it is marked as a legal hikers' lot. Usually a 6-inch yellow diamond marked with a black "H" designates such places. Unfortunately, this means hikers do not always gain close access to trailheads. A written list of hikers' parking areas is available from any of the visitors centers, where you can also purchase trail maps. Camping is allowed only in the public campgrounds (reservations recommended) or in lean-to shelters (first-come, first-served). Dogs are allowed on leash only, and may not swim in bodies of water. For more information, call the park superintendent at 914-786-2701.

Besides the two chapters offered here, I also recommend the following:

• **Bear Mountain.** Park at the Bear Mountain Inn (fee) and inside the inn walk up to the second-floor parlor for a look at the oil painting of Rip Van Winkle hung over the stone fireplace large enough to roast whole game. Back out in front of the inn, follow the red-marked 1777 trail left toward Hessian Lake, where it shortly meets up with the white-marked Appalachian Trail. Follow the Appalachian Trail markers along the lake shore, then across US 9W, past statues and memorials, past Trailside Museum at the site of Fort Clinton to the Bear Mountain bridge. On your return you can circle Hessian Lake. Although much of this walk follows paved trails, it is full of a book's worth of Revolutionary War tales. Next, drive to the back of the parking lot to pick up Seven Lakes Drive. Motor to Perkins Memorial Drive, which will bring you to the top of Bear Mountain for the 360-degree view and an informative stone tower.

• **Popolopen Torne.** The nearest legal parking for this small, bald peak is at Bear Mountain Inn, making this a long hike. There are fabulous, 360-degree views.

• **Claudius Smith's Den.** This is a large rock shelter cave used by the infamous outlaw. Park at the Tuxedo train station, cross the tracks, and follow the red-dot trail south, cross the Ramapo River on a footbridge, go under the Thruway, left on Grove Drive, and then climb the steep Harriman plateau to a wide view. Continue until a right turn onto the red-dash trail, followed by a left on the blue-marked trail. The cave overhang is on your right.

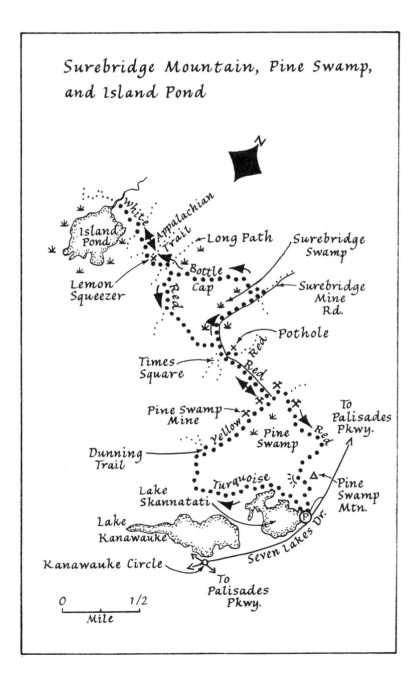

Surebridge Mountain, Pine Swamp, and Island Pond

Island Pond

White

Appalachian Trail

Long Path

Surebridge Swamp

Lemon Squeezer

Bottle Cap

Surebridge Mine Rd.

Red

Pothole

Times Square

Red

Red

Pine Swamp Mine

Pine Swamp

To Palisades Pkwy.

Dunning Trail

Yellow

Red

Turquoise

Pine Swamp Mtn.

Lake Skannatati

Lake Kanawauke

Seven Lakes Dr.

Kanawauke Circle

To Palisades Pkwy.

0   1/2
Mile

Surebridge Mountain, Pine Swamp, and Island Pond

Location: Harriman State Park
Distance: 7 miles
Owner: State of New York

Mountain bogs, rosebay *(Rhododendron maximum)*, deep, dark hemlock forests, deep, dark iron mines worked in the 1800s, and a sparkling lake make this a full-day excursion. It is important to follow directions and trail markers with care. There are a lot of paths here, both marked and unmarked. With each intersection you have the choice of continuing on or returning home via your own route.

Access

From Tiorati Circle drive 2.5 miles south on Seven Lakes Drive to a large parking lot at Lake Skannatati. Hikers' parking is at the bottom of the hill on your immediate right.

Trail

Begin on the Long Path. Be certain to follow the turquoise markers along the lake shore, as there are other paths here. One of the trademarks of Harriman is its open, mixed deciduous, Hudson highland forests dominated by oaks and floored by spring-blooming woodland sedges, most commonly *Carex arctata,* lapped past open bedrock knolls green and gray with lichens. These are bright-sunny, open, friendly seeming woods, sometimes with nothing at all growing on the forest floor. Bedrock and glacial till close to the surface of the acidic soil limit the availability of water and cause the wide spacing between the oaks. Likewise, the dry soil cannot support a tall shrub layer. When shrubs do occur they are usually limited to patches of mountain laurel and a covering of lowbush blueberry and of huckleberry, both of which grow no taller than your knees. These heaths, blueberry and huckleberry, are able to obtain moisture from the humus through their roots. With all those oaks Harriman Park is not a woods to visit in a gypsy moth infestation year. These oak woods inhabit the dry crests. In cool moist ravines find hemlock.

You may encounter a burn area anywhere in these woods but especially over deciduous crests and on the sides of summits where leaf litter accumulated. Typically, old burns are studded with the silvered skeletons of dead oak and mountain laurel and populated with a lush growth of fresh greenery: hay-scented fern, St. Johnswort, sweet fern, grasses, cat briar, mosses, and lichens. You will not find a deep burn among the sedges; fires only top-singe these.

At the intersection turn right onto the old woods road of the yellow-marked Dunning Trail. Bedrock outcrops leveled and smoothed on their north sides and plucked on their south sides by glaciation are strewn with more angular blocks of erratics, rocks carried by the ice and dumped. The same weighty glacier that rounded this bedrock ground down the entire Hudson Valley landscape of gentled hills.

Pine Swamp is one of a number of bogs in the area perched within a glaciated bedrock bowl that holds water. This sphagnum marsh is a great place for botany, pond life, birding, frogs, or just sitting by the open water on rocks gazing at the spatterdock and white water lilies. Shadows of turkey vultures pass overhead. Turn a sweet gale leaf's underside in the sun to see the sparkle of gold resin dots. Admire the leatherleaf, sheep laurel, sedges, and marsh St. Johnswort *(Hypericum perforatum)*. Out in the bog among the smothering sphagnum and fine-leafed tendrils of cranberry grow the embedded vases of carnivorous pitcher plants *(Sarracenia purpurea)*. Back on the trail, watch the slope on your left for a hill of tailings camouflaged beneath leaves and hemlock needles. Leave the trail and climb steeply to Pine Swamp Mine. Actually, this is the eighth and largest cut; the other, smaller seven are just north. The pool of water fills a seemingly bottomless shaft. Walk into the long, echoing cavern in the side of the mountain.

Back outside, handle some of the black tailings at the dump, weighty with magnetite. Rust marks the iron, and the biotite and muscovite mica glitter. Pine Swamp Mine ore was carted past the nearby mining community village (foundations are across the trail) to a kiln about a half mile east of the Greenwood furnace for reduction and then smelted at the furnace. The huge stack of Greenwood furnace can still be seen along NY 17 at Arden, restored by the Orange County Historical Society (for information, phone 914-351-4696). The resulting pig iron was used in the manufacture of stoves, hardware, cannonballs for the War of 1812, and the devastating Parrot artillery gun of the Civil War.

Continue on the yellow trail to a brook crossing. Another small mine cut is just upstream. Continue along the trail as you enter the vast hemlock forest that furs all the ravines of this area. Soon you see another mound of mine debris on your right. At the intersection, turn right to see, on your immediate left, the mine—a straight cut with no roof, filled with water coated with a film of foxfire. This is one of a number of bioluminescent organisms by that name. Face the water's surface one way and the foxfire looks like nothing more than the unhealthy murk of oily rust water. Move and watch how the surface sheen changes to an iridescent amber glow and then leaps into a sparkling, three-dimensional, living gold.

Head west along the Arden-Surebridge Trail, marked by a red triangle within white paint, through the hemlock-clothed valley on the old Surebridge Mine Road. A large erratic and fireplace mark the multiple-trail intersection known to urban hikers as Times Square.

A short side trip down the red-dot-on-white-marked Ramapo-Dunderberg footpath on your right will shortly bring you to a ledge of bedrock. As you climb it, watch carefully on your left for a chimneylike half cylinder 4 feet wide and 8 feet deep. This is a glacial pothole. Usually, potholes are formed by streams where gravel whirls for millennia scouring a round, potlike depression in the stream's bedrock. The lack of any streambed at this site precludes that typical formation. It has been postulated that a stream once ran on the Wisconsin glacier. As the meltwater coursed into a crevasse at this spot, it scoured out the pothole high up on Fingerboard Mountain. In fact, if you climb up on the top of the ledge the undulating bedrock looks for all the world as though smoothed by a rushing current. Return to Times Square and take the combined turquoise-marked Long Path

Like other green plants, pitcher plants (Sarraccnia purpurea) *photosynthesize their own food, but because they are not rooted in mineral soils they must rely upon their carnivorous habits to supply them with the small amounts of nitrogen, phosphorus, and potassium necessary for survival. These nutrients are unavailable in bogs.*

and red-triangle-within-the-white of the Arden-Surebridge Trail along Surebridge Mine Road. When the trail markings soon turn left, keep straight on the unmarked old mine road. Emerge from beneath dark hemlocks and rosebay to Surebridge Swamp, a sphagnum bog awash in tiny red sundew *(Drosera rotundifolia)* and cottongrass *(Eriophorum virginicum)*. Like the pitcher plant, the sundew eats insects. Once trapped on the glittering, sticky dewdrops, the hairy, spoon-shaped leaves fold over their prey for digestion. North America's smallest dragonfly, the bluebell, also lives here.

Travel a long, narrow ridge of hemlock and rosebay through the marshland. When the wetland ends on your right, find a small mine hole filled with water. This is one of the shafts of the Civil War–era Surebridge Mine. There are more up the slope. Doesn't look like much? Many of these innocuous-seeming holes are thousands of feet deep. In 1880 alone, 458 tons of ore were taken from Surebridge Mine.

When the wetland ends on your left, watch for a vague footpath crossing. This is Bottle Cap Trail. Turn left, cross the brook that drains Surebridge Swamp, and follow the bottlecaps nailed into the trees. The trail is also marked with cairns, stacks of three or four rocks. On this seldom-used trail, you must often sight from marker to marker; great fun! Bottle Cap leads up and over the wild ridge-rills of Surebridge Mountain, and you get to know the terrain on its own terms rather than along a stone mine road. It is more like a guided bushwhack. Pass through beautiful open and rocky oak and sugar maple woods floored in sedges. At one point you pass a small, shallow round hole in the ground. This is a charcoal pit, a common sight throughout the mountains of the Northeast. Several cords of wood cut from the spot were slowly roasted into charcoal, then sold for home use or to fuel early, pre–Civil War iron furnaces. Bottle Cap Trail next angles down the mountain slope through an extensive and gorgeous hemlock forest. Three bottle-caps signal the trail's end at the bottom. Turn right on the Long Path and Arden-Surebridge Trail. Cross a moist strip just north of which you see the main body of a marsh called Dismal Swamp. The Long Path turns right, but you keep straight following the red-triangle-within-the-white markers. This runs into the white-marked Appalachian Trail at the Lemon Squeezer. Play around the narrow cleft in the granite cliffs, then proceed to Island Pond (which means you do *not* go up Lemon Squeezer) along the Appalachian Trail, following the white markers. You can see the lake sparkling up ahead through the hemlocks. Island Pond and Hessian Lake are the only natural ponds in Bear Mountain and Harriman State Parks. After a long haul through woods and hills, hikers rest bemused with wonder at the open stillness of this deep lake. In summertime, you will meet through-hikers making their way from Georgia to Maine, or thereabouts. Ask for their trail names; each has one.

To return, take the white-marked Appalachian Trail back to Lemon Squeezer and bear right onto the red-triangle-within-the-white. Follow these markers back to Lake Skannatati on a variety of roads and footpaths. First you climb steep Surebridge Mountain, then pass a marsh on your left. Next skirt the edge of a burn. Turn right onto Surebridge Mountain Road, through Times Square (do not take the red-dot-in-the-white), and head down the hemlock valley on the mine road. You come to new territory at the intersection with the yellow-marked Dunning Trail. Keep straight on the red-triangle path past more mines on your right onto a footpath. Pass foundations on your left. Climb the oak and beech woods of Pine Swamp Mountain, passing several charcoal pits. There is a great view of the lakes and hills from the summit before a steep descent to the parking lot.

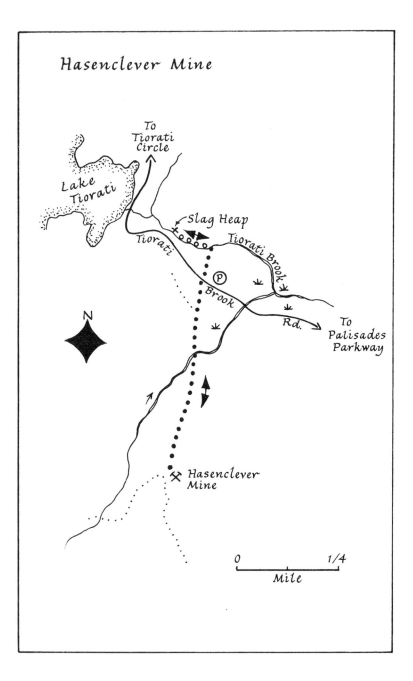

Hasenclever Mine

To
Tiorati
Circle

Lake
Tiorati

Slag Heap

Tiorati

Tiorati Brook

P

Brook

N

Rd.

To
Palisades
Parkway

Hasenclever
Mine

0   1/4
          Mile

Hasenclever Mine

Location: Harriman State Park
Distance: 1 mile
Owner: State of New York

This walk is for those times when children pester you that they *really* want to see an iron mine but cannot go far.

Access

From Tiorati Circle drive east on Tiorati Brook Road (closed in winter) 1.6 miles to parking in a dirt lot on your left.

Trail

Walk right uphill on Tiorati Brook Road about 50 feet to the trailhead on your left. This is the red-cross trail (white paint with a red cross). Keep straight on an old woods road for half a mile. "This is one of the oldest roads in the park," you explain. "Built in 1760."

"That's before the Revolution!"

"Yep. In fact, it's on the maps George Washington had his mapmaker, Robert Erskine, make for the war."

"What's this cement thing?"

"That post is an old town marker for the road. This is Hasenclever Road."

"To Hasenclever Mine!"

"Built by Baron Peter Hasenclever."

"Who was he?"

"He wasn't really a baron, they just called him that. He was a businessman, an *entrepreneur*. Came here from Germany but he worked for a mining company in England."

On your right you will find foundations. The mine is on your left where the old woods road forks. The bedrock outcrop was cut away and the quarry pit is now filled with rusted water. Frogs flee into the pool with a cry and a plunk.

"That's *it?*" screech the kids. "It's just a hole full of water."

"It *is* 100 feet deep," you say. "Let's look for the tailings." They are on your right, and downhill of that are straight parallel ditches and beds built to carry a railroad that was never finished. On the return, watch for a fork where you will bear right.

"Want to look for remains from the slag pile from James Brewster's iron-smelting furnace? He owned the mine after Baron Hasenclever. They called it Orange Furnace."

Cross Tiorati Brook Road and continue across the field on the red-cross trail. At Tiorati Brook bushwhack upstream to the foot of a series of cascades.

"The furnace is gone, but slag might still be in that thicket of barberry bushes. Watch out, they have thorns."

"Look at this rock! It looks like lava!"

"That's slag left over from smelting. Look at this black glassy one."

You can learn more about Hasenclever Mine in *Vanishing Ironworks of the Ramapos,* by James M. Ransom.

Schunemunk Mountain

The Megaliths. These and the rest of Schunemunk's durable, pink quartz conglomerate were formed when fishes and trees first appeared in the world— a time when the Hudson Highlands were already ancient.

Schunemunk Mountain

Viewed from the east, Schunemunk is a supine mountain creased by streams. Viewed from the west it is a long plateau (some even call it a mesa) fringed with a long and level cliff. Schunemunk's shape comes from its own unique, highly resistant conglomerate cap that supports a barrens forest of pitch pine and red and scrub oak.

A steep-walled island rising above the valley floor, the unique bedrock of Schunemunk actually continues southwest past Greenwood Lake into New Jersey. The pink conglomerate caprock is perhaps most similar to Shawangunk conglomerate, but it was formed at the same time as the Catskills. Schunemunk shares vegetation and climate characteristics with both the Shawangunk and the Hudson Highlands. There simply is nothing else quite like it.

This rock is pink because it originally formed on a tropical, sand beach when the continent drifted near the equator. Three hundred fifty million years ago mountains the size of today's Swiss Alps towered to the east. They are known as the Taconics. Erosive mountain streams sluiced off these mountains carrying and rounding quartz pebbles. These led into a shallow sea where the dumped pebbles sank cocooned within a soft bed of mud and sand rich in hematite that gave it a pink color, much like the warm pink sands of Florida and Bermuda today. This mass later solidified, compacted, uplifted, and folded into the conglomerate cap of Schunemunk.

Schunemunk's cap has resisted erosion, preserving layers of softer shale and sandstone beneath. As you hike later in the Hudson Highlands, watch for diagnostic glacial erratics of this pink pudding stone dragged from Schunemunk.

Schunemunk

Location: Mountainville
Distance: 6 miles
Owner: Mountainville Conservancy of Storm King Art Center
and Star Expansion Industries

A large mountain, Schunemunk has many trails to choose from. This chapter describes one of the shorter loops to the summit. If you do not care to climb mountains, try following the description below, but just before the railroad crossing keep on the road to make a loop along the mountain's foot to Baby Falls.

Access

At the stoplight intersection of NY 300 and NY 94 in Vails Gate, proceed south on NY 32 for 4.2 miles, passing the stoplight for NY 107 to Cornwall, until a sign on your right for Black Rock Fish and Game Club. Turn right here onto Orange County 32. Drive 0.1 mile to a left turn onto Taylor Road. Go 0.2 mile over the Thruway and another 0.1 mile to parking on your right, courtesy of Star Expansion Industries.

Trail

From the parking site, walk toward the New York State Thruway for about 30 feet. Use the map to help you follow the white trail blazes to the railroad tracks. Head straight into the woods, where your ascent begins.

The trail follows the northern rim of Dark Hollow. At the end of the scree, the trail begins to switchback uphill. When you hear the sound of falling water off to your left, you may wish to carefully (without trampling plants or snapping saplings or branches) bushwhack over to see the small series of cascading steps of water. The brook waterfalls down the steep slope to join Dark Hollow Brook

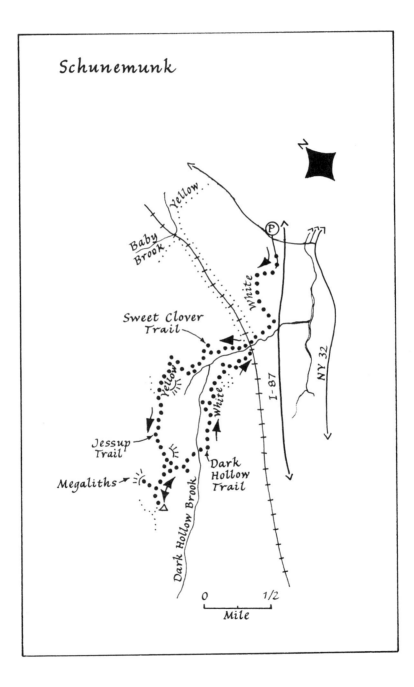

Schunemunk

below. You will feel an immediate microclimate change. The air is cooler and moister, and of course the thick growth of hemlocks makes it very dark.

Return to the white-marked Sweet Clover Trail and climb steeply. As you near the crest, the forest becomes more stunted than ever. Schunemunk conglomerate begins to show up in the trail: blocks of rounded pink and white quartz pebbles within a gray and pink-purple quartz "cement."

Climb. At Sweet Clover Junction turn left on the yellow-marked trail up conglomerate bedrock past stunted pitch pines rooted within cracks. On Schunemunk's crest find conglomerate pebbles, some large enough to be termed cobbles, of white quartz sheared clear in half by the last glacier as it lumbered over the mountain. Some of the exposed bedrock has been rounded into wavelike forms. Pass a perched wetland growing woolgrass sedge *(Scirpus cuperinus),* button-bush, and sheep laurel.

Each outcrop leads higher. Finally emerge out to a grand view of Newburgh Bay, strewn with white sails on weekends, from the Beacon-Newburgh Bridge to Danskammer Point, beyond which the Hudson curls and disappears. See Pollepel Island within the North Gate of the Hudson Highlands, Little Sugarloaf, and the Fahnestock plateau. Keep on to another outcrop where the view stretches west, north, and south to encompass all of Orange County and points far beyond. If the sky is clear, it is easy to pinpoint the major features of the Shawangunk in one glance: Mohonk's Sky Top and Eagle Cliff, the Trapps, Mill Brook Mountain, the long, high plateau tilting up to Sam's Point, followed by the southern Shawangunk into the Kittatinny. The high peaks of the Catskills include Slide Mountain behind the high white cliffs of Mill Brook Mountain in the fore-ground.

At Dark Hollow Junction, keep straight on the yellow trail past pitch pine barrens and stunted red oak. A sign painted on the bedrock points west (right) toward the Megaliths. Follow the white paint dots across the bedrock to what I consider the prize-winning view. South-ward stretch the rumpled Kittatinny (Lenape for "big mountain") of New Jersey near the Pennsylvania border (tower on top; highest point

Some of the pitch pines (Pinus rigida) *growing on the exposed Schunemunk bedrock look like bonsai. Each dwarfed pine grows ringed by a cushion of soil largely made up of the tree's own fallen and decayed needles.*

in New Jersey). These are simply a continuation of the Shawangunk under a different name. The continuous high ridge along the western horizon is part of the southern Catskill plateau. You have a clear view of all the Shawangunk, Catskills, and Marlboro Hills, and of the massive Galaxy air transport carriers of the Air National Guard Reserve at Stewart International Airport. At your feet is a cleft, filled by Barton Swamp, and the rise of Schunemunk's west ridge. The hill beyond that is Woodcock Hill, and south (left) is a perfectly molded hill called Round Hill. Both of these are klippes of Hudson Highlands granitic gneiss.

The Megaliths are a group of impressive conglomerate knobs that pulled away, it seems, from the main body of bedrock. Here you will find mountain-ash festooned in fall with red berries. One narrow cleft between megaliths grows thick in winterberry. Be very careful as you explore the "caves."

Return to the yellow trail and turn right for Schunemunk's summit, at 1664 feet one of the highest in the region. The 360-degree view is somewhat obscured by the summit's canopy. Return to Dark Hollow Junction and turn right onto Dark Hollow Trail, marked in white with a black center. This infrequently used path leads steeply downhill over ledges and through soil pockets that may be muddy after a rain. Pick your way across Dark Hollow Brook at a gorgeous, cold-paradise of a place where the gold-shot water lazes past green ferns over quartzite pebbles. There is no bridge here, just steppingstones and stepping-roots. In autumn the yellow-gold cinnamon ferns and the fallen red tupelo leaves float on the water's surface and gem the bank.

Dark Hollow Trail leads away from the stream to traverse a short but sweet blueberry and scrub oak habitat growing on a south-facing slope, akin to a Hudson Highlands habitat. From here you gain another grand view of the Hudson River east to the south Taconic range. Then walk downhill again through mixed oak and hickory woodland. Cross a stream that flows southward (away from Deep Hollow), turn left on the trail, and watch in the woods on your right for an old charcoal pit, approximately 3½ feet deep by 15 feet wide.

Pass many old trails and roads, witness to extensive past use of the mountain. Keep on the marked trail, which turns into an old road. Disappointingly, the road does not carry within Dark Hollow, as its name suggests, but along its dry southern rim. You hear the cascades roaring below and see a few token hemlocks. The old road continues in its own direction as you follow the marked footpath. At the foot of the mountain finally get a taste of Dark Hollow. Just before the railroad tracks, watch on your left for an unmarked trail leading off into the hemlocks and upstream. Follow this into the dark and thick hollow centered on water rushing over rocks. The steepness of the ravine precludes you from going far; and remember the tremendous damage even a small amount of trampling can inflict upon hemlock ravines. Cross the brook on boulders, being careful as they may be slippery. Follow this to the railroad tracks and retrace your steps on the white-marked trail back to your car.

Delaware Valley Lowlands

The Neversink River at Neversink Preserve

Delaware Valley Lowlands

The ecology and history of these park sites are focused on the Delaware River. For someone from the Hudson Valley, where commerce, transportation, history, flora, fauna, and folklore are all centered on the Hudson River, coming here is like crossing over into another country. Watersheds predetermine the course of human activity more than we sometimes realize.

The word "Delaware" comes from Sir Thomas West, third Lord De la Warr, governor of the Virginia colony. The river, bay, and the various Lenape bands living along that river were named after him. The parks in this section lie near the heart of traditional northern Lenape country.

The history of the Delaware & Hudson Canal runs a common, invisible thread through these parks and links them to sites in the Hudson Valley lowlands. Folk balladeer Rich Bala sings this song borrowed from an old Erie Canal tune:

> *I've traveled all around the world, and Lackawaxen, too.*
> *Been cast on desert islands, been beaten black and blue.*
> *Fought and bled at Bully Run; I wandered as a boy.*
> *But I'll never forget the trip I took from Honesdale up to Troy.*
>
> *So it's tramp, tramp, and tighten up those lines.*
> *Watch the playful horseflies while on the mules they climb.*
> *Whoa back, duck your nut, forget it I never shall*
> *When I shipped aboard a canawling-barge on the D&H canal.*
>
> *We shipped on board at Wurtsboro bound for old New York.*
> *The first thing that they rolls aboard is a barrel of black rock pork,*
> *From Ellenville to Eddyville they fed it to poor-old me,*
> *Then they boiled a barrel and leftover pork*
> *And they served it up for tea.*

And the cook we had upon the decks stood six feet in her socks.
A bosom like a box car, her breath would open the locks.
Well, she fried some pork for breakfast
And a chunk for luncheon, too.
And when it came time for dinner she'd prepare some black rock stew.

Well, when we got to Kingston-town with Sally, Jack, and Hank,
We greased ourselves in tallow fat and slid off on a plank.
Now Sally's in the police gazette and the rest of the crew's in jail,
And I'm the only son of a sea cook left to tell the tale.

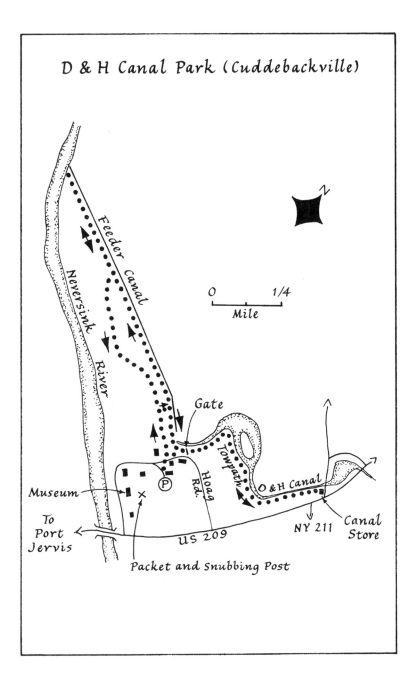

D & H Canal Park (Cuddebackville)

Feeder Canal

Neversink River

Gate

Towpath

O & H Canal

Museum

Hoag Rd.

P

To Port Jervis

US 209

Packet and Snubbing Post

NY 211

Canal Store

0   1/4
Mile

N

Delaware & Hudson Canal Park

Location: Cuddebackville
Distance: 3 miles
Owner: County of Orange

Looking for a way to bring Pennsylvania anthracite coal to a new market in New York City, Maurice and William Wurts hired thousands of Irish immigrants to build by hand a 108-mile-long canal from Honesdale, Pennsylvania, to Kingston, where the coal was loaded onto barges at today's Sleightsburg Spit on the Hudson River (see chapter 39, "Other Parks"). The Delaware & Hudson Canal Company operated from 1828 until 1898, doomed by the more efficient railroads.

This park maintains the only relict section of the D&H Canal still regularly supplied with water.

Access

The park is right in Cuddebackville—north of Port Jervis on US 209 or west of Middletown on NY 211. Where US 209 crosses the Neversink River turn north onto Hoag Road. There is a sign here for the park and for the Neversink Valley Area Museum. Follow signs for parking at the visitors center. The trails are always open. The museum is open noon–4 PM, Thursday through Sunday, March through December, or by appointment. The museum's phone is 914-754-8870. Be sure to get a copy of the self-guided D&H Canal tour.

Trail

It might be best first to walk back to the museum at the Leura Murray Center and enjoy the exhibits and view the stone abutments where the canal was carried over the Neversink in a wood aqueduct. I often enjoy a walk better once I have some understanding of the history of an area. But there are also plenty of times when I am impatient and head straight out onto the trail, letting the real thing speak for itself, reasoning, "Time enough to visit the exhibits later." Even if you visit when the museum is closed, you must go behind the Leura Murray Center and see the replica of a packet, or passenger, boat and the real snubbing post. Once I knew what a snubbing post looks like, I started to see them elsewhere in my travels around the region. There were hundreds of these things when the canal operated, but only a handful, by comparison, are preserved today. The majority have vanished to locales unknown. When in place, about one-third of the granite pillar sticks up above ground, which puts perhaps 6 feet buried underneath. These are big and heavy stones made of imported, high-quality, dense, and hard granite, yet they are nothing compared to the weight of fully loaded coal boats. The earliest canal boats on the D&H were called flickers, 20-ton vessels. The later boats increased to 40 tons and, eventually, to 145 tons. When any of these tied up to the snubbing posts, locking stretched the manila lines dirtied with quartz Shawangunk grit and cut smooth grooves right across the granite. Every snubbing post I have seen is scarred by these awesome marks.

From the visitors center, you can cut across the lawn to the left of the building and on up to Hoag Road. Turn right uphill. Two feet before the first building—the old grocery store—turn left past a locked gate with a "No swimming" sign. This takes you past waters emerging from the pines (leaking from the canal), past the embankment of a bridge that carried the canal and into a white pine plantation. On your right you can see the slope of the feeder canal that still supplies water to the D&H Canal. Watch for the herd path by a seepage pool on your right that leads up to a weedy footpath along the rim of the feeder canal.

This feeder system is filled with lazy-moving, green water from the Neversink. Feeder canals were required because of the constant locking operation along the system that flowed water down the canal. Once the canal was abandoned, the Neversink Light and Power Company used the feeder canal to produce electricity for Port Jervis, Middletown, Monticello, and Liberty from 1902 until 1948. The hydroelectric plant was that boarded-up building in the weeds you

Tramping the towpath

passed before you parked your car at the visitors center. The electric company in turn abandoned its plant when a flood washed out its reservoir. If not for this company, however, the feeder canal never would have lasted long enough for us to enjoy today.

Watch your footing on this canal wall. The way is narrow and plants hide the edge. A misstep could send you rolling down the steep embankment or into the canal.

The feeder canal corners an elbow and you can see the Neversink glistening nearby. The walk is shaded, peaceful, and reminiscent of the old canals of England. Soon you come to an overflow gate used to safeguard the canals from high floodwaters. Across the canal rosebay blooms in July beneath hemlocks. A well-tramped path continues from this point until the feeder guard gates at the breached dam on the Neversink. Please watch your footing around this area. Do not walk on top of old and crumbling masonry. Above the dam, a beaver lodge rests in the center of the river.

Head back the way you came. Cross the overflow gate and take the side trail to your right off the canal down to the woods road. Follow the dirt road through hemlocks and sugar maples into the white pine plantation. At the seepage area and the herd path, now on your left, climb back up the embankment and turn right to see the rest of the feeder canal. The whole thing simply disappears underground at a small grate. You can see signs of high-water spills over the top. Cross carefully on rocks to a mown lawn, actually the roof of the underground feeder canal. At a wooden bridge you can see the Neversink's pilfered water welling up into the D&H Canal—and immediately leaking out into a brook. Cross the bridge and arrive at the famous D&H Canal, covered in a blowing green cloth of duckweed.

You are standing at the site of lock 51. It used to be in front of the garage, but in the 1940s it got filled so the car in the garage wouldn't fall into the lock when it backed out. This was one of 108 locks and represented the boundary between the Neversink and Summit sections. The white building with the garage was a grocery store where patrons could buy baked goods from Mary Casey and Martha Van Inwegen, proprietors, while they waited for the bottleneck at the lock to pass their packet through. Casey and Van Inwegen were especially known for their deep-dish rice custard pies so scrumptious that lock 51 was better known as Pie Lock.

The next white house was the lock tender's home. As the canal curves left, follow the D&H Canal heritage trail along the original towpath. Besides the history and colorful folklore of the canawlers to be learned, the towpath is a good place to come with a tree field guide if you want to learn species. Vigorous specimens with leaves close to the ground and at eye level have suckered up from cut stumps. The trail ends at the canal store.

Neversink Preserve

Location: Godeffroy
Distance: 1½ miles
Owner: The Nature Conservancy

The Nature Conservancy calls this 206-acre preserve one of the "Last Great Places" on its list of the Americas' and Pacific Rim hemisphere's 75 most biologically diverse habitats. As the resident caretaker says, "If you don't like what you're seeing, walk a couple of yards." Undoubtedly the surrounding area is likewise diverse, and in my travels around the western section of Orange County I have noticed a rich cross-mixture of northern and southern species that is characteristic of the southern Shawangunk.

Yet Neversink Preserve is the cream of a good crop. Not by any means is it virgin growth. Two railways passed through the property that speeded the delivery of the clear-cut timber to faraway mills. But the wooded section has been left to itself at least from the 1930s, a rarity in a fertile and populated valley. More recently it was a private hunting and fishing preserve, so it was left alone long enough for it to mature into a natural showcase of regional flora and fauna. It contains the rare, the common, and the endangered. It is a pocket missed by progress and improvement where survive the wisdom and natural heritage of our landscape. This is the place to come to when you want to do some serious land-listening. If you are a student of woodland or old field botany, there could be no better classroom.

It is an unassuming piece of land. There are no astounding views. The entrance parcel was until recently a farm and the rest is mostly level floodplain. The Neversink River at this point is a world-class trout stream, swift-moving, clear, shallow, and wide.

Access

From Cuddebackville, cross the Neversink on NY 209 headed toward Port Jervis and within a few hundred yards take your second left turn

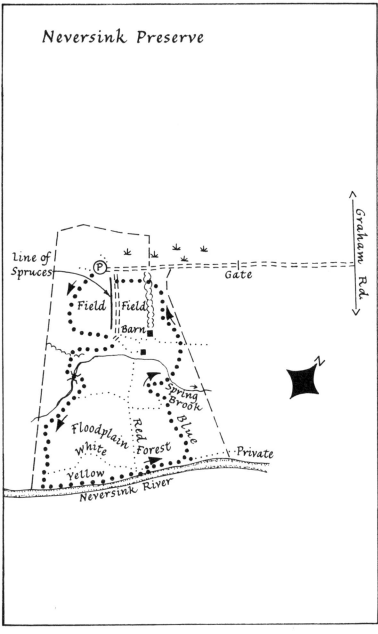

Neversink Preserve

Line of
Spruces

Gate

Graham Rd.

P

Field

Field

Barn

Spring
Brook

Floodplain

White

Red

Forest

Blue

Yellow

Private

Neversink River

The Neversink River contains globally endangered and rare mussels. Neversink is a Lenape word that Ruttenbur translated as "at the point, corner, or promontory," and that Beauchamp believed meant "highlands between water."

onto Old 209-3. Go for 0.7 mile to where the road forks. Take the left fork to Graham Road. Turn left onto Graham Road. The preserve entrance will be on your right in about 200 yards. Drive in along the long old railroad bed past a gate and an active beaver pond. Watch for turtles and herons. This was a narrow-gauge railway that hauled timber from the clear-cut Neversink Valley for loading onto barges in the D&H Canal on the northwest side of today's US 209. Leave your car in the designated parking area. No dogs are allowed. The preserve is open every day all year, from dawn to dusk. For more information, call the caretaker, 914-858-2883, or the Lower Hudson Chapter office of The Nature Conservancy, 914-244-3271.

Trail

From the parking area, walk straight ahead on a mown path. This takes you through successional fields of goldenrods and saplings alternating with wet woods of gray birch being succeeded by red maple. At the four-corners intersection turn right through the goldenrod field into a woodland of red maple and yellow birch mixed with some black cherry. Cross Spring Brook.

Not only are there many different canopy species of trees, but the understory, shrub, and herbaceous layers are also highly diverse. As you walk you can find black oak, red maple, and yellow birch (especially by the stream) shading a herbaceous layer of blueberry, huckleberry, cinnamon and hay-scented fern, Canada mayflower, princess pine lycopodium, and mosses. You will see ironwood, pignut hickory, hemlock, basswood, tupelo, spicebush, white pine, and beech, partridgeberry, fringed loosestrife, deer-tongue grass, and Virginia creeper all within a short distance of one another. Sugar maple appears on (very) slightly higher ground. These are odd combinations of wet and dry species.

Cross a brooklet coated in duckweed; pass bushes of winter-berry and speckled alder. Off to your right wave fields of corn. As you approach the Neversink, tulip-tree, sycamore, and ash appear, along with many, many more species too varied to list here.

A side spur leads to the river's edge where red maple and yellow birch arch over the swift-moving Neversink. On the opposite shore rises the slope of Wurtsboro Ridge of the southern Shawangunk thick in rosebay rhododendron beneath hemlock. The two banks, a stream's-width apart, grow different woods. This is due to a difference in slope microclimate. The opposite side faces north. Its annual mean temperature is slightly lower than that of the south-facing shore, and its soil is moister. Under such conditions, hemlock and rosebay can outcompete any other flora.

A short exploration of the stream rocks in the current reveals a plenitude of life. A stream provides innumerable microhabitats for plants, insects, leeches, mites, sponges, crustaceans, flatworms, earthworms, rotifers, and other creatures, not to mention the larger animals such as fish and shore-basking frogs. Take a single rock, for example. It has an edge that faces upstream into the brunt of the current. An animal that lives here must be adapted to holding onto its substrate, like the flattened water penny and the rows of caddisfly nymph houses. No need to go anywhere looking for food, just open the mouth into the current and let the stream bring what it will. The rock has a downstream edge where the rock's bulk provides near-complete protection from the current in a microeddy of a backwater. This is an extremely valuable resting, breeding, and living site within the ripping current. The rock has two sides and a top over which the current races, or perhaps it sticks up into the air, an important site for breeding adults and emerging larvae. Mosses and other plants on top of the rock can create additional places to live. The rock has a bottom perhaps propped between other rocks, leaving a cave of a space for crayfish, salamanders, fish, and hellgrammites. Or perhaps it is sunk into mud, or sand, or silt, or clay, or any mixture of these. Each variation provides a different habitat exploited by often disparate species. One simple rock; innumerable niches. You might find the nymphs of mayfly, stonefly, blackfly, fishfly, and various beetles. Be certain to replace any rocks you handle exactly the way you found them.

Follow the yellow-marked trail along the river's edge over sands deposited by flood. The trail turns into the woods, crosses an old stream channel, and turns right into lovely, mature woods. Watch the river for merganser ducks. When they are not diving for fish they preen and rest on the larger boulders. Listen for osprey and watch the cobbles along the shore for the lilting Louisiana water thrush.

The trail leads through groves of beech, white pine, and hemlock. The yellow trail ends. Turn left on the blue-marked trail into woods of towering white pines and red oak underlain with woodland sedge. At the fork, bear right across Spring Brook. The path leads you back into the field- and new-forest patchwork where deer bed in the daytime within dense cover. Just beyond the black walnut stand on your right, cross a narrow sand embankment. This is the bed of another narrow-gauge railway that transported the raw resources from the Neversink Valley to the D&H Canal. Keep straight past intersections and through a classic abandoned hayfield. Bring some flower field guides and seat yourself in the botanical classroom (although the redwings will not appreciate your studiousness).

Follow straight through to the next field and to the entrance driveway where your car is parked.

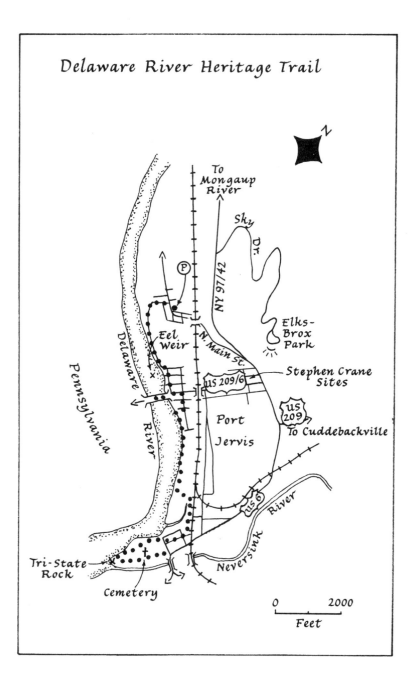

Delaware River Heritage Trail

Delaware River Heritage Trail

Location: Port Jervis
Distance: 4 miles
Owner: City of Port Jervis, maintained by the
Minisink Valley Historical Society

This is an urban walk of historical buildings, waste places, cemeteries, and post-industrial decay through a declining railroad and canal town along the Delaware River. It is as close as many American children and adults ever get to nature. Why is it in this collection of nature walks? Because the commonplace is as important as the rare. The urban habitat is a growing part of the same community web that includes diminishing wild forests and wetlands. Both make up the region's ecosystem.

Peter Osborne, of the Minisink Valley Historical Society, designed this walk through the city to take in the historical and natural sights, including the longest local walking path along the Delaware River. The trail is 75 percent handicapped accessible. This is the one walk where I advise you to carry some cash, so you can purchase an ice cream cone or enjoy a cup of coffee along the way.

Access

From the stoplight intersection of US 209/US 6 South with NY 97/NY 42, take NY 97/NY 42 north for 0.3 mile to the blinking caution light. Turn left onto West Main Street. Go for 0.4 mile across the railroad tracks to a right on Old West Main. The 1793 stone house, Fort Decker, 126–133 West Main Street, and its small parking lot are on the corner. For more information, call the Minisink Valley Historical Society, 914-856-2375.

Trail

Pick up a trail guide on the porch of Fort Decker. Find the state education department plaque in front of the building. See the orange rectangle painted on the post? That is your trail marker.

Follow along West Main on a sidewalk of bluestone quarried from the Catskills and hauled on the D&H Canal to your first left onto Ferry Street. A backward glance reveals high Mounts William and Peter, of Elks-Brox Park, a place to visit upon your return. Ferry Road curves into River Road. The Delaware flows before you, Pennsylvania on the opposite shore. Walk the grassy bank, actually a dike that protects the city from flood. Both sides of the road grow a vast array of wasteside flora, some native, others alien, all hardy and opportunistic species able to establish themselves in the difficult growing conditions of poor soil, scant water, and full-glaring sunlight. Most are either edible, medicinal, or both.

Gray birch, black cherry, and black walnut are often found colonizing the edges of neglected agricultural fields. The conditions here are identical, and here are the same species. Ailanthus, or tree-of-heaven, sumac, and black locust are colonizers of the most degraded of places. Along the dike where conditions are slightly richer, find the medicinal sundrops *(Oenothera fruticosa)* and inkberry *(Phytolacca americana),* bouncing bet *(Saponaria officinalis)* for soap, chicory *(Cicorium intybus)* for coffee. Did I call them *waste* places?

At Flo-Jean restaurant, the original tollhouse, leave the trail to walk out on the bridge along the pedestrian pathway. Upstream is an eel weir, a large V of stonework. The Atlantic Ocean may be 255 miles away, but every fall hundreds of mature female eels swim downstream headed for the Sargasso Sea to spawn. Back at the restaurant, if you want a snack, now is your last chance to buy something. The trail leads around the second block and back to the river by way of the dike.

The trail follows the dike through a park. Gray squirrels forage on the lawns. Woodchucks, the eastern marmot, graze on grasses and stems, seldom straying from the safety of their burrow entrances. English sparrows fly up from the playing field and perch within the chain-link fence. Starlings strut along the lawn looking for insects to eat. Both of these were imported and deliberately released by Europeans homesick for the sweet birds of their native lands. Aggressive, adaptable, gregarious, boisterous, and omnivorous, they outcompete native species for nesting and feeding sites. At the end of the ball field, take the road to your right that leads down off the dike and toward the river. Cottontail rabbits sit by the road edge.

Stroll the cinder bed past silver and ashleaf maples. Side paths lead down to the water. At an intersection with several roads, turn sharply left and climb up onto the highest railbed. This was the Erie Railroad bed and is still used by Conrail, so keep well away from the tracks. Approaching trains are surprisingly quiet and can travel at high speeds. All along the bed grow the purple flowering knapweed and the yellow spikes of the medicinal mullein *(Verbascum thapsus)*.

Continue straight until the markers signal a right turn into a neighborhood. At the corner, turn left and enter the Laurel Grove Cemetery. Pass towering white pine specimens that would make a timberman drool, hemlocks, and horticultural specimens of rhododendron. Almost, this is the best part of the walk, quiet, tended, and trash free. Continue through to the horrific I-84 overpass. Truly, now, here is the way many Americans experience the out-of-doors, through their car windows. Port Jervis, with all its woes, and the lovely Delaware River, with all its riches, whiz past in a few blinks. At the dead end stands the witness monument that recognizes Tri-State Rock at the water's edge, surmounted by a benchmark, as the boundary of three states. It doesn't sound like a big deal now, but it settled a long and nasty border war. The world-class trout stream, the Neversink, enters the Delaware unobtrusively on your left, looking like nothing more than a quiet cove. Start your return by following the Neversink past large sassafras trees, plenty of basswood, and the sound of water tinkling over another eel weir. Bear right through the cemetery.

There are any number of routes back to your car. If you are still feeling energetic, you could walk East Main Street/US 6 past fine architecture and graveyards to the Stephen Crane sites at Sussex and Canal Streets, then onto West Main Street. Or you can meander the neighborhoods, or retrace your steps along the Delaware. I found the shortest return is straight through the main line of the Erie Railroad. A Conrail cinder bed parallels the rails the entire length of the city. When you pass beneath a bridge, take the first road on your left. Decker Fort awaits you on the corner.

Mullein leaf tea and the concentrated flower oil are used mainly by contemporary herbalists for lung congestion—and were once used for the same problem in cattle.

Want to see where you've been? In summer, drive up West Main Street and turn left onto NY 97/NY 42. Go 0.6 mile and turn right at a sign for Kolmar Laboratories onto Sky Drive. Follow this up the mountain, past Kolmar, all the way to the end at the flagpole atop Mount Peter. This park was developed during Port Jervis's gilded years. Today it is subject to vandalism and loitering, so often the lower gate on the road is locked. The walk in from that point to a view is about 0.5 mile. It's a good view. Port Jervis honks and hollers below. The Delaware makes a broad sweep through a floodplain that separates two major geological units: to your right the Appalachian plateau, to your left a long ridge that northeast of Port Jervis is called Shawangunk and southeast is called Kittatinny. The tower on top of the Kittatinny ridge is located at High Point State Park, the highest point in New Jersey (1803 feet above sea level).

Feeling drained of spirit? Visit nearby Mongaup River.

Mongaup River

Location: Hawk's Nest
Distance: 4 miles
Owner: State of New York

The last stretch of the wild Mongaup River is a world-class trout stream popular with kayakers. A few white-water miles upstream Mongaup has been dammed to create the Rio Reservoir and shunted into a hydroelectric plant. This walk follows the white-water section.

The valley was purchased by New York State in 1990 to protect critical, habitat for the endangered bald eagle. Since disturbance in winter can lead to fatality in eagles, Mongaup Valley Wildlife Management Area is closed to hikers and everyone else from December 1 through March 31. The public can view bald eagles in winter by driving along the roads near the reservoirs, especially the north end of Rio Reservoir, and watching from inside their cars. For the walker, visit Mongaup in July when the vast, hemlock-shaded valley blooms with an understory of rosebay.

Access

From the stoplight at the intersection of NY 209 North and NY 97 in Port Jervis, drive on NY 97 west for 6.6 miles past Hawk's Nest, the winding mountain highway along the Delaware River that you may recognize from automobile advertisements on television, and downhill. Park in a dirt pull-off on your right immediately before the bridge that crosses the Mongaup River. No camping is allowed. If you have questions, phone the Fish and Wildlife Unit, New York State Department of Environmental Conservation, New Paltz, 914-256-3090.

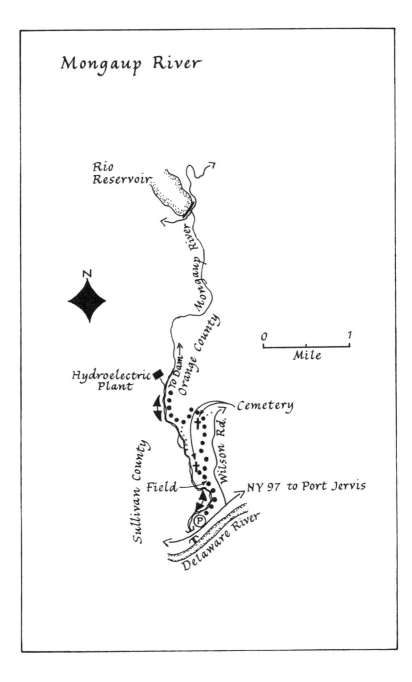

Trail

None of the mostly level, old woods roads in this valley is marked, but it is easy to find your way so long as you keep the direction of the river in your mind.

From the parking pull-off you can see an old road across the street that leads down to the Delaware, which you are free to explore. Behind the state education department sign follow a footpath to the woods road and the D&H Canal stonework mentioned in the sign. Do heed the warnings that the river's wildness is subject to sudden flow increases. The hydroelectric plant upstream swells its discharge of water into the river without warning during periods of heightened electricity need. Typically, the river is lower in morning than in afternoon.

Follow the road lined with a shrub layer of rosebay *(Rhododendron maximum)* beneath hemlocks, the combination so dense and dark that nothing grows beneath the entire slope of the great laurels. This is the shrub of the mountains from Maine to Alabama, most common in the Great Smokies and other Appalachian hills, yet it is difficult to find in the Hudson Valley. I know of a few sites on the west bank (none occurs on the east) of the Hudson Valley where rosebay occurs; a fabulous hidden swamp in Sterling Forest, secret pockets within Harriman State Park, a rare stand on Crow's Nest, and the few scrawny individuals of the Shawangunk. The Delaware River watershed in New Jersey, Pennsylvania, and the Kittatinnys is the abode of rosebay. Orange County falls within this watershed along the Neversink and Mongaup Valleys.

Yellow birch and red maple now and then punctuate the hemlock-rhododendron forest with light. Fallen rhododendron blossoms and rosy buds collect in eddies of the cool and loud river. Follow the road. Mongaup carries its shout a short distance away. The road leads to a field. St. Johnswort *(Hypericum perforatum)* is a European immigrant, the tall plant with the gold-yellow flowers in July and August. It has been said that perhaps no other herb is surrounded by so much folklore as St. Johnswort.

The road gets a bit vague here. Follow straight the way you were headed into the riverside woods. Soon you arrive at an old

The wide evergreen leaves of rosebay (Rhododendron maximum) *have rolled edges and are arranged in a whorl that serves up a nosegay of large rose or white flowers, magnificent and shining in the hemlock shadows.*

cemetery enclosed by a stone wall, a dark and cool, moldering rest beneath hemlocks situated on a well-drained spit of land between ravine wall and river. The Knight family stones date from the 1840s to the 1880s. The bodies were laid facing east (toward the rising sun, a burial tradition). The little stones are each grave's footstone. The inscriptions face west so that you, the visitor, will not traipse over the graves to read the markers.

With your back to Mongaup, look up the ravine wall. See the old road, continuing? You can bushwhack straight up the steep slope or, better, walk back toward the St. Johnswort field—site of the old farm—and scout out the road at its beginning. The hemlock trunks grow so densely that the road looks like a ribbed tunnel. Watch for the corpse plant, also known as the parasitic and pale Indian pipe. Hardscrabble farms like those of the Knights never got wealthy. Hillfolk living on 10 to 15 acres that contained some pasture, some cropland, and some unusable rocky fields, they supplemented their income with timbering, quarrying (although not here on the Mongaup), hunting, fishing, and trapping. Near the farmhouse grew a patch of garden. Most of these farms scraped along until the water companies bought them up.

The road strikes away from the ravine rim to follow the foot of the upper slope, but you can still hear the Mongaup below. You may notice another, vaguer road banking up the hill. Do not follow it. Keep straight on the main track past good stonework of walls. The ravine lip cuts close and away again while the road takes you on a level and easy saunter.

Arrive at a T-intersection with another old woods road. A right turn will bring you to Wilson Road, forming a possible loop back to the parking lot if you do not mind walking a short distance along NY 97. If you want to continue along the Mongaup River, then turn left and look immediately on your left beneath the hemlocks for a small forlorn and forgotten graveyard. None of the tombstones is marked. Minisink Valley historian Peter Osborne explains that this is an earlier cemetery, perhaps from 1830 to 1850. The deceased may have been too poor for carved stones, or perhaps, as Mr. Osborne describes in his pamphlet "Silent Cities: Graveyard Art and its History," they were "slaves . . . buried apart from their owners in unkempt areas without fences. Their markers are usually blank . . . Native Americans, who stayed after their lands had been purchased by settlers, are sometimes found in these separate burial grounds as well."

The old woods road now switchbacks steeply downhill. At the foot of the ravine, the left fork leads through beautiful white pine and hemlock streamside woods that are a pleasure to explore. The right fork soon brings you to a stone foundation, all that remains of a bridge over the Mongaup River. The road becomes vaguer; once the hydroelectric plant comes in view, it vanishes altogether.

If you are feeling energetic, you can continue up the Mongaup by bushwhacking. All you have to do is follow the river (disinherited of half its water). The hemlock woods are fairly open but the ground is uneven, making for difficult walking.

The return is either back the way you came, up to Wilson Road, or up to Rio Reservoir. Whichever your route, *do not* try to bushwhack along the river back to the cemetery. This route is *extremely* dangerous and long. Use the woods roads.

Hudson Valley Lowlands

Rondout Lighthouse from Sleightsburg Spit at the confluence of Rondout Creek and the Hudson River

Hudson Valley Lowlands

The parks within this section all lie on land settled and well used by humans since ancient times. Ground construction on the banks of the Hudson River and its major tributaries without fail reveals evidence of human habitation over millennia. The Lenape name for today's Hudson River is lost, but the Mahikan, "Mahikannituk" and its variations translate as "tidal river of the Mahikans." The war- and small-pox-stricken times of the 1600s and 1700s soaked the coveted, fertile soil of these lowlands in the blood of hundreds of Esopus, Dutch, Huguenot, and English peoples.

The Esopus were a large band of Lenape living along today's Esopus Creek and the surrounding region. Europeans named them Esopus, after the place where they lived. They called themselves *Lenape,* "The People." Whereas Europeans insist the Lenape and all Native Peoples traveled from Asia across the Bering Strait, traditional Lenape insist they originated in the Hudson Valley, or nearby, born from a sacred red cedar tree planted by the Creator on the back of a primordial Turtle. Archaeological evidence proves the Esopus Lenape civilization flourished in its homeland for at least 4000 years, and probably twice more than that amount.

The Huguenots were Protestant refugees from Catholic France. First they fled to the Palatinate or Paltz region of Germany, then many of them fled war again to America. When those who settled in Kingston fought in the Second Esopus War, they passed through the Wallkill Valley and fell in love with it. In 1677, a dozen Huguenot men purchased 144 square miles from the Esopus Indians.

The sites you will visit in this section are as varied as the region's history. You'll find lighthouses, quiet forests, creeksides, steep ridges, hemlock ravines, and the Hudson River itself.

Warwick Park

Location: Warwick
Distance: 1 mile
Owner: County of Orange

I f you find yourself in the Warwick area wishing for a breath of fresh air, visit the small hemlock ravine of this county park. Whispering Trails was originally built by the superintendent of maintenance, Mickey Petrillo, and a group of Youth Conservation Corps kids. As the youngsters worked in this ravine on the lower slopes of Warwick Mountain, and ate lunch beneath the hemlocks, they heard many whisperings of water and trees. They are the ones who gave the trail its name.

Access

At the convergence of NY 17A and NY 94 in the village of Warwick, drive east on NY 17A toward Greenwood Lake for 1.3 miles. The park entrance is on your right. Follow signs for the senior center and the golf course. On your left pass the driveway to the senior center, a plaque, and a flagpole, and take your next immediate left to parking above and behind the senior center parallel with fairway 11. The park is open dawn to dusk. Dogs are allowed on leash. For more information, call the park superintendent's office, 914-986-1169.

Trail

Walk back to the main road and uphill about 50 feet to the trailhead on your right. Do not take the dirt road that crosses the brook. Whispering Trails is the brookside footpath. Follow it upstream through sugar maple woods. There is some poison ivy along here. Watch for three large slabs of local stone in the trail. This is actually a bridge in the old farm style of the early 1900s, wide and strong enough to carry loaded wagons, but the brook no longer runs beneath it. The bridge covers an abandoned channel nearly perpendicular to the current

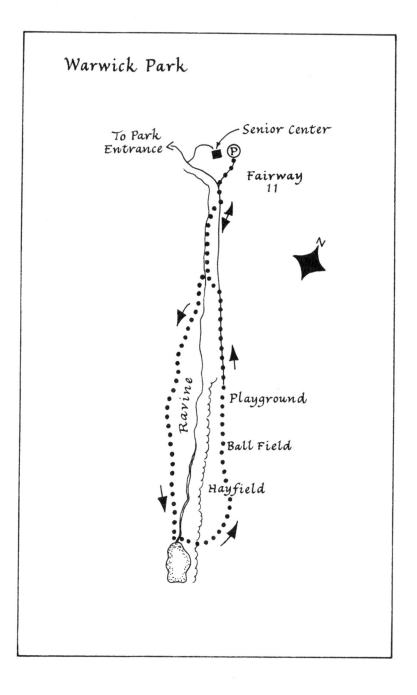

streambed. A bit farther on the trail brings you to more big rock slabs. Both of these bridges were built by a farmer who once owned the land. Warwick Park is made up of three to four old farms purchased in the 1970s. Streams, even little brooks, move. They do not stay put beneath their bridges. They are like squirming snakes, their coils undulating now this way and now that way downhill; you just need to watch them over a long period of time to see this pattern of movement. Such power enables even little brooks like this one to erode deep and wide ravines.

The width of the stone slab bridges shows the original width of the farm road. The brook has eaten away most of the road itself. When you recross the brook on steppingstones, leaping across at times of high water, you can see the farmer's old retaining wall that attempted to channelize the current and hold the brook to its bed. This prevents bank erosion, for a time, sometimes even for centuries. But sooner or later flood takes the bank and the snake undulates on, cutting across floodplain or into ravine.

Barbed wire strung between trees separates the far brook edge from an adjacent field of old pasture. This kept cattle out of the ravine. But the trees kept growing and swallowed the barbed wire within their bark. Fortunately for them, the farmer did not wrap the wire around the trunks. As they grew, the wire would have severed their circulatory systems of upward moving sap, girdling and killing them.

Watch for false Solomon's-seal *(Smilacina racemosa)*. The graceful, reclining stem of wide and shiny leaves terminates in a foam of white flowers that ripen into salmon berries spotted in purple. The true Solomon's-seal has larger flowers along the stem and is usually overall a smaller plant. False Solomon's-seal berries can be eaten raw, but too many will give you diarrhea. Native Peoples used them sparingly as a food seasoning. The young shoots can be steamed and eaten in the spring, and the roots, once leached of their bitterness, can be boiled like potatoes.

At the fork, bear right across the brook (look for black-nosed dace minnows) and into the hemlocks. These conifers grow here because of the cool, moist microclimate. They can outcompete any other tree species at this site under these conditions. The one thing they can not survive, though, is an introduced insect pest called the wooly adelgid. These minute, fuzzy white insects suck the sap of hemlock trees. Millions of them sucking year after year eventually kills the trees. Hemlock has been eliminated from much of its former ravine habitat in the lower Hudson Valley. The adelgids are sucking the life out of these lovely hemlocks at Warwick Park, too.

The trail climbs along the top of the ravine wall through a stunning, dense, and dark hemlock hollow. The contrasted brightness of some beech and black birch only accentuates the hemlock shadows. At the next fork bear left, keeping along the ravine lip. A ravine like this is useless to a farmer. The brook could run a mill if the year-long flow were steady, which in this little brook it is not. The steep slope is dangerous to cattle. It is not worth planting and it is difficult to timber. However, this ravine, and all of the park land, was lumbered out 30 years ago. About all a hemlock ravine is good for, other than peeling the hemlocks for tanbark, is to run a road along the rim. Most of the hemlock ravines I have seen in the Hudson Valley have such old roads.

As the ravine levels out and the microclimate warms and dries, the hemlocks give way to sugar maple with beech, black birch, and other deciduous trees. Here the farmer did build a dam for a barnyard pond. Cross the earthen dam and peer into the water at the myriad insect life on top, beneath, and above the pond.

The trail leads out to a hayfield. Turn left to follow the wagon ruts along the field edge past grasses and the tall flowers of summer, both alien and native, including ironweed, milkweed, Queen Anne's lace, and many of the goldenrods. Look up in the air over the field about 20 to 30 feet at the domain of whole squadrons of large, predatory dragonflies, expert fliers whose bodies have been the model for fighter jet design. If you visit after a frost, these insects harmless to humans will be absent.

As you approach the ball field, there is a narrow view of the southern Shawangunk on the horizon. In the hazy summer that ridge looks every bit its old name of Blue Mountains. Pass the playground and walk downhill along the paved road. Pick up the trail again after the road has split and rejoined at a gate. Enter the woods on your left along the ravine lip beside yellow birch trees. Keep straight to return to where you began.

Plum Point

Location: Newburgh
Distance: ¼ to ½ mile
Owner: State of New York, managed by Orange County

The main attraction at this 108-acre park is the stupendous view of the North Gate of the Hudson Highlands. Come at low tide to enjoy the sand beach.

Access

From the intersection of I-84 and US 9W in Newburgh, head 4 miles south on US 9W through the city, past Downing Park (designed by Calvert Vaux in memory of his mentor and partner, Newburgh's own Andrew Jackson Downing, America's first landscape gardener and inventor of the first uniquely American architecture), past the turnoffs at Broadway for New Windsor Cantonment and Washington's Headquarters (where the United States of America was largely shaped), and straight on toward (but not to) the hills of Black Rock Forest on the horizon. Immediately past the Toyota car dealership on your left and before the bowling alley, turn left through the gap in the divided highway onto Plum Point Lane (may be unmarked), which takes you over the railroad tracks. For information, call 914-457-3111.

Trail

You smell the river before you see it. At the prized, natural beach of dark Highland sand, the view is outstanding. The stories that go with the view would fill a book. Each hill, island, and water has a name and each at least one story, if not several tall tales.

Look straight across wide Newburgh Bay at bald Little Sugarloaf, prone to fires. There are a number of Sugarloafs in the Hudson Valley. They all get their names from the Dutch, who likened their pyramidal shapes to the packed sugar cones, called *suycker broodt,* that once were hung by a string in the middle of Hudson Valley colonial tables. The

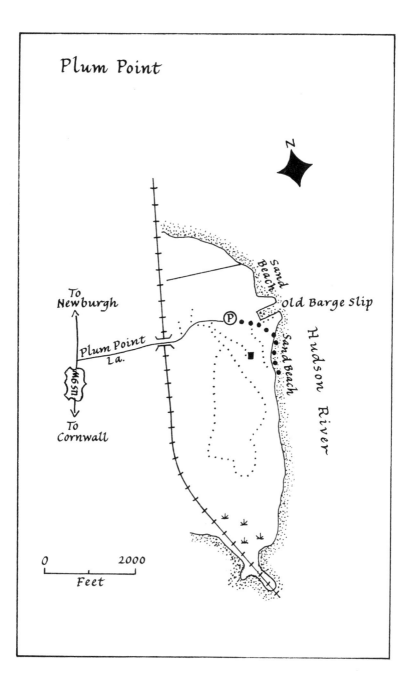

Plum Point

space in the Hudson River between Storm King and the opposite mountain, Breakneck Ridge, is called the North Gate to the Hudson Highlands or the Wind Gate—in old Dutch, *Wey Gat*—for sailing ships a treacherous entrance into the tide-tricky, narrow Highlands reaches. This is a water gap, a place where the river eroded its canyon directly counter to the grain of the Appalachians. It was here that glacial debris formed a natural dam and flooded the postglacial landscape with meltwater clear to today's Albany, a vast water termed Lake Albany. Some of the sand deposits on today's nearby slopes are ancient alluvial fans deposited into that lake.

A Victorian-era fabrication tells how the Great Spirit, angered by the Indians' wanton killing of animals, broke open that dam with one ax blow. The ensuing flash flood scoured out the deep and narrow Hudson channel through the Highlands. Scientists attribute the fjord to glaciation that carved out a riverbed deeper than the mountains are tall. At the foot of Breakneck, you can see the brick housing of the tunnel heading where the Catskill Aqueduct resurfaces from beneath the Hudson River.

The shore of Newburgh Bay and its attendant points of land, where major tributaries enter the Hudson, were heavily used by various Native Peoples throughout human history. Within Newburgh Bay, sloops—freight ships peculiar to the Hudson River—used to gather in the shadow of Sloop Hill in Cornwall by the hundreds, waiting for the tide to turn to catch a favorable wind through the North Gate for points south.

Pollepel Island stands just without the North Gate, some say named for Polly Pell, or (more likely) Dutch for pot ladle, where drunken sailors (off their ladle) were ditched by their captains, left to sober up while their mateys sailed north to the trading post at Beverwyck (today's Albany). It is said they sobered up fast, what with the spirits that haunted the place. Moonshiners set up shop there in the late 1800s. Several fascinating characters built homes and lived on this island, including a woman who believed she was the queen of England and sang opera into the North Gate winds. Francis Bannerman, a gunrunner whose stockpile of arms and powder exploded one night (after it had been sold to New York State),

Wide Newburgh Bay. A view of the North Gate of the Hudson Highlands from the old barge slip at Plum Point. Storm King is to the right, Breakneck Ridge to the left.

destroyed the 1908 replica of the family's castle in Scotland. These are the ruins you see. Pollepel Island is now owned by New York State, part of Hudson Highlands State Park, but remains off limits to the public.

Within Newburgh Bay on a foggy September morning Henry Hudson anchored the *Half Moon* and allowed his men ashore to hunt for wild grapes, where they ran afoul of the local Native folks. From that incident evolved the tragic Victorian love story of the Indian woman Manteo and the Dutchman Jacobus van Horen: Manteo saved Jacobus from her vengeful kin, but Jacobus betrayed her love, and she killed herself at the falls of Indian Brook in present-day Cold Spring. Newburgh Bay slims to a point on the western shore. This is Danskammer Point, perhaps the most sacred place in the Hudson Valley for traditional Munsee and Esopus peoples. For centuries, after disease, war, and change forced them from their homeland, these Natives continued to return year after year to gather upon this ceremonial rock, today surmounted by a power plant.

Atop the Beacon Mountains—the tallest hills in the view—pyres were maintained during the Revolution in case it was necessary to summon the militia. Likewise atop the Beacons, the Wappinger Indians were swindled out of their land by two enterprising Dutchmen. From Danskammer Point the Hudson River runs north straight out of sight to Poughkeepsie. This long stretch was named *Lange Rack* or Long Reach in Robert Juet's journal (which survived the ravages of time, whereas most of Henry Hudson's own journal did not). Juet was a mate on board the *Half Moon*. A sailing ship can navigate this impressively long straight sailing course with only one setting of the boom.

Looking out at this abundance of forest, hill, and water, you have no hint that you stand near two large and noisy cities. There is little sign of Beacon and none of Newburgh. The only sounds come from wind and river waves, some droning of boats, and, very distant, the muted traffic on US 9W.

Trails from the interpretive center on top of the bluff lead through areas quarried for sand and gravel first for a brickyard and later for a building-supply company. Black locusts are colonizing the dried, infertile soil. These are leguminous trees, which means that nodules on their roots contain blue-green bacteria that transform atmospheric nitrogen into nitrates and nitrites—soil fertilizers. If you open one of these nodules you will find it pink with hemoglobin to scrub the oxygen that inhibits the nitrogen-fixing process. The locust tree is also able to send up new trees from its roots, and thus can spread more easily than other trees, which depend on seed germination. In the shade of the locust, humidity is trapped, and plants are shaded from the desiccating sun and protected from wind. Sugar maple, tulip-tree, elm, and hickory saplings sprout beneath the pioneering locusts, eventually healing the damaged land, transforming it back into forest.

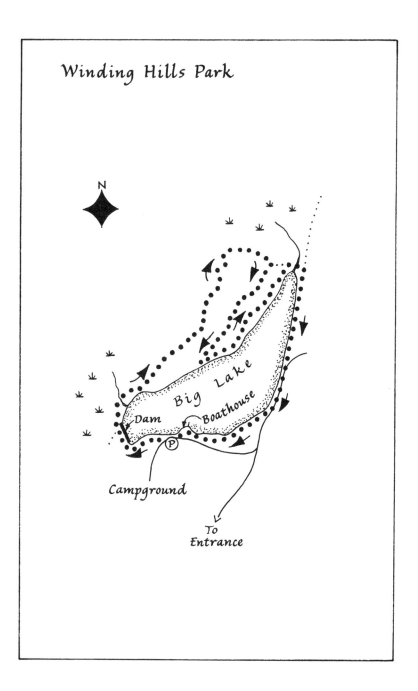

Winding Hills Park

N

Big Lake

Dam

Boathouse

P

Campground

To
Entrance

Winding Hills Park

Location: Montgomery
Distance: 1 mile
Owner: County of Orange

Winding Hills is a pleasant park for a stroll in the woods. The variety of soil and vegetation habitats makes it a good site for botanizing and bird-watching. Visitors also enjoy camping, boating, and fishing. The trail system is well marked and easy to follow. Unfortunately, there is a lot of noise from overhead airplanes.

Access

From the traffic light intersection of NY 17K and NY 211 in Montgomery, proceed west on NY 17K, across the Wallkill River, for 2.5 miles. Turn right onto Old Route 17. In 0.1 mile the entrance gate booth to the park will be on your right. Follow signs to park at the boathouse. The front gate is locked at 9:45 PM. Dogs are allowed on leash. For information, call 914-457-5950.

Trail

Walk toward the campground along the paved road, and shortly bear right onto a dirt road through hardwoods mixed with some hemlock. Mostly they are oak: chestnut, red, black, and white. There are also sugar maple, black birch, and pignut hickory. Since they are present together for comparison, this is a good opportunity to learn how to distinguish among these species.

As the dirt road curves downhill, watch the verge for tick trefoil. I have found it blooming here in late August, purple-edging the road. It still surprises me that a flower so exotic-looking can mature into such ugly sticktights. Watch on your right just before the dam for the important medicinal horse-balm *(Monarda punctata)*. The square stem indicates it is a mint. It has a peculiar smell, a cross

At Winding Hills Park

between celery and mint, some say lemony, that attracts a multitude of bees. Naturalist Peter Kalm complained in 1747 that the citronella smell always gave him a headache. Use a magnifying glass to look closely at the tiny flowers: yellow and lavender with projecting male anthers like a dragon's horns and a fringed lip of a petal.

The road becomes the red-marked trail, which will bring you to an earthen dam at the lake outlet, a popular place for anglers. Climb uphill into open woodland. The trail leads into hemlocks with no undergrowth. These abruptly end at the bottom of the hill. Bear right at the fork, keeping on the red trail. When the trail bends right, look on your left for farmers' rock piles. These accumulated when one of the previous owners annually cleared his fields for plowing, by hand. One of the piles is heaped on bedrock, the better to save valuable soil space for planting. Stone walls to either side of the trail are further evidence of former farming use.

Straight trees in the bottomland to your left make up an ash swamp. There are many large and magnificent trees along the trail. Some white ash stand at the stone wall crossing, and beyond them some vaselike sugar maples. Beyond these the forest turns into a lovely woodland of black birch.

At the next intersection, turn right for a loop along the Heritage Trail. (If you want to shorten your walk, keep left to cut off this loop.) The path follows the ridge line before descending toward Big Lake and returning. At the intersection, turn right and cross the brook that feeds Big Lake. As early as January in a mild winter, skunk cabbage can be blooming in the brookside silt.

By autumn the extensive Virginia creeper ground cover of the woodland turns scarlet and can be seen distinctly. Turn right at the dirt road. Painted turtles haul out to sun themselves on floating logs in the lake. Follow the dirt road until a right, then turn here onto a pretty grass-covered path along the lake shore. Here grow arrow-wood, swamp blueberry, and red-osier dogwood, shrubs of sunny wetland edges. If you stand still in a sunlit spot, a clear and light blue damselfly may alight on you for a rest. They neither bite nor sting. Keep straight at the paved road and pick up the trail again in a short while. This leads along the remainder of the lake shore to the boathouse where your car is parked.

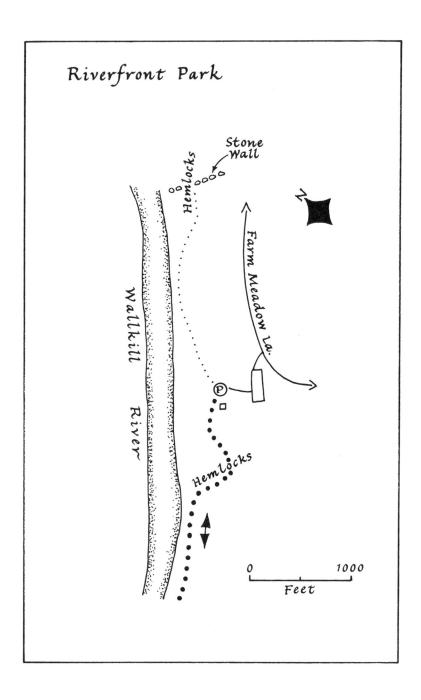

Riverfront Park

Stone Wall

Hemlocks

N

Farm Meadow La.

Wallkill

River

Hemlocks

P

0   1000
Feet

Riverfront Park

Location: Walden
Distance: ¾ mile
Owner: Town of Montgomery

In 1986, environmental quality bond funds allowed the municipality to purchase this charming, 35-acre, 4000-foot frontage on the lazy, tree-hung Wallkill and preserve it for us all to enjoy. The visible lack of nearby houses and roads preserves the illusion of a visit back into Orange County's pastoral, agricultural past.

Access

From the stoplight in Walden at the intersection of NY 208 and NY 52, go south on NY 208 for 1.7 miles to a right turn onto Bailey Road. There are signs here for a restaurant, an inn, and the town park. Go 0.5 mile to a right turn on Farm Meadow Lane. Go 0.2 mile to the park entrance on your right. Park downhill beside the river. It is open dawn to dusk for 9 months of the year. Snow closes the parking lot in winter. Dogs are allowed on a leash. For information, call 914-778-5651.

Trail

The picnic area beneath large, graceful swamp white oaks is the trailhead for the south trail headed upstream, an unmarked dirt and gravel road. Pass over the knoll of hemlocks down to the wide Wallkill riffling over shallow ledges of broken bedrock. This leads into pleasant, cool, mixed deciduous woods of sugar, red, and silver maple, red and white oak, ash, hickory, elm, and hop hornbeam. On the opposite bank the view is curtained by more woods and the green gleam of farmers' fields. Wallkill is a silty river, but wade out and turn over rocks within the streambed. You will find nymphs of mayfly and stonefly, among many others, and armies of crayfish. In the warm summertime the pools by the bank are awash in what appear to be dead crayfish of every size, but these are just shed skins.

Huge carp live in the Wallkill. In summer you might see them flopping about near shore spawning or notice dark dorsal fins cutting the pools. At this time you can approach closely before they notice you. You might even catch one by hand, but they are sheer muscle and slippery. Carp come originally from Asia and were introduced into the Hudson River in the late 1820s.

Where in April the trail skirts a muddy area of skunk cabbage, watch for wild leek *(Allium tricoccum)*. The smooth green leaves push up on purple stems just as the shadflies appear. Munch a leaf or two as a natural insect repellent that will exude from every pore. Wild leek senesces or goes dormant and disappears by June.

You may walk this trail for 2000 to 3000 feet before the end of town property. Watch for an obstruction (probably a cut tree laid across the trail), beyond which you should not trespass.

Silver maples overhang the bank of stinging nettles and pale jewelweed. The Wallkill has undercut the bank and felled a few. Little blue herons perch in the dead limbs. Kingfishers flash past on the wing and plovers search the silted shore. Dairy cows shoulder down to drink at the river, standing knee deep in the green grasses. Under the heat of summer cicadas buzz, and carp slap the warm, brown water. What a gem this little park is!

Hemlock Ridge
Multiple Use Area

Location: Plattekill
Distance: 1½ miles
Owner: State of New York

This 52-acre forest is good for discovery and for getting lost along the complex of logging, hunting, and off-road-vehicle roads that sometimes shift with each year. Things start out simply enough, but the farther in you go, the deeper in you get. Bring a good sense of direction.

Access

From US 9W in Milton, turn west onto Ulster County 10, also called Milton Turnpike. Go 4.1 miles to a left turn onto South Street. In 0.8 mile, a narrower South Street turns left off the main road, so watch for this carefully; follow South Street. Go 1.7 miles, where South Street becomes Lewis Road. Continue 0.4 mile more to the parking entrance on the left.

Trail

The dirt road leads through a mixed deciduous forest of oaks, red maple, black birch, and hop hornbeam. Soon hemlocks appear on your right, a dark, secretive woods with an open forest floor. Leave the trail here, step up to the stone wall, and carefully search with your eyes for an orchid called spotted coralroot *(Corallorhiza maculata)*. It grows among the hemlocks just beyond the stone wall. The leafless, single, slender stems, about 8 inches high, rose turning to gold at the top, are easily missed even when crowned by the tiny flowers in late July, so if you venture into the hemlocks, place your feet with caution. (You will also be leaving state land.) Do not even think of picking these flowers. Rather, kneel down on a level with them. The waxy blooms are gold with purple edges and spots, the center lobe white

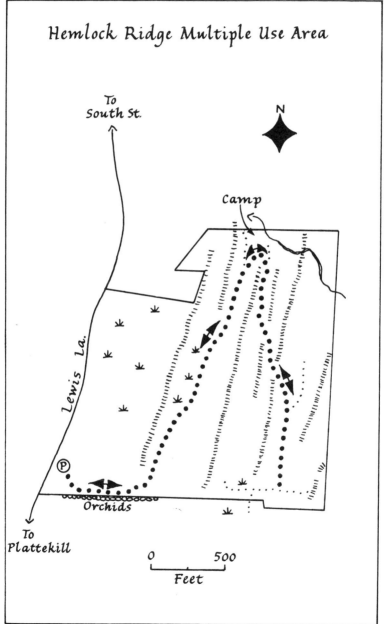

Hemlock Ridge Multiple Use Area

with purple spots. This is a northern orchid more common in Canada but also found in mountainous areas of the United States. It grows here because of the cool, mountainlike microclimate. It contains no green pigment and so is unable to photosynthesize its own food like other plants. Instead, orchids feed on decaying plants or animals in the soil, but cannot absorb this organic material directly. Orchids rely upon an intimate and complex cellular or mycorrhizal association between their roots and the soil fungi. If you dig up an orchid and transplant it to your garden, the soil fungi will die, and so will the orchid.

Return to the dirt road. Hemlocks appear within the deciduous woods. Blackberry grows along the trail where sunlight shines through openings in the tree canopy overhead. On your right rise cliffs topped with hemlock, the main feature of this preserve. The astringent tannin in hemlock has long been used medicinally by Native Peoples. Hemlock tea bathed on a wound puckers it closed and stops the bleeding. Taken internally, it stops hemorrhaging and diarrhea. Munched raw or taken as a weak tea, hemlock needles supply vitamin C. Hemlock has been used to induce abortion, but has dangerous side effects, including serious peritonitis. This is a good example of the importance of proper dosage and preparation in herbal medicine. One of my favorite uses is for a refreshing bath. Make a very stiff cup of hemlock needle tea (let it steep for at least 2 hours) and add this to a hot tub. Ahh.

Hemlocks grow and tend to persist on slopes in the Northeast where it is cool and moist year-round. In traditional ecological terms, such a growth is called a climax forest: self-perpetuating and stable, barring catastrophe. It is so dark beneath their needles that few, if any, shrubs or herbaceous plants can grow. A dense hemlock canopy, like the one here, allows less than 20 percent of a day's full sunlight to penetrate to the forest floor. This lack of sunlight enhances humidity and coolness. In such shade only sapling and seedling hemlocks are found, but even they cannot flourish without sunlight. Although extremely shade tolerant, a shaded hemlock grows slowly. Trees no thicker than a broom handle may be 50 years old. If a blowdown or a bulldozer opens the canopy to let in the full sunlight, that 50-year-

Nowadays, hemlock is limited to cool, moist ravines; sheltered, moist flats; ridgetop pockets; and north-facing slopes. In these habitats it is lord and ruler. This is not the poison hemlock that Socrates drank; that is a European streamside herb. This is an American tree.

old hemlock will shoot up, growing faster in a few summers than in all its previous years. This is one of the adaptations that make hemlock a dominant species. The fallen needles also acidify the soil, further precluding other competitive species.

On the left spreads an extensive woodland pool in springtime. In April, this is an important breeding site for amphibians. Continue uphill over smooth bedrock. Bear right at the fork past a mixture of upland and lowland plant species.

The farther you explore, the more obscure the trail becomes, with more branches of old logging roads. Off-road vehicles create new paths. There are many dark ledges to investigate. If you take the left fork up the wet hill, and at the downed trees keep straight through the hemlocks as the road curves left uphill (see the retaining wall of rocks in the roadbed?), and at the next fork keep right, still uphill, you will be on the main trail that travels along the upper part of the preserve past hemlocks, wet woods, and many ledges. This is old farmland. At one point the road leads uphill through an old lane lined on both sides by stone walls. These trails may be muddy in spots after a rain or in spring. There are no views.

Pass clumps of cottonwoods, upland woodlands recently grown in from abandoned farmland, older woodlands, and stands of black birch. At the T-intersection, turn right for more hemlocks and wet and swampy red maple woods on top of ledges. These are excellent woods for wilderness camping, with plenty of nooks and crannies for campsites and quiet. A good sense of direction will allow you to choose trails that circle back to your car, or you can try bushwhacking (be very careful around ledges), or simply backtrack the way you came. You might startle an owl out of its hemlock cover. You will not hear it, since owl flight is soundless; stay alert with your eyes. The diversity of wet, dry, shady, and sunny habitats is a joy to explore. There are caves in the ledges and purple monkey-flowers in the logged clearings. The trails seem to run off state land onto unmarked private property, so be careful not to wander miles out of your way. Enjoy, and find your way back safely.

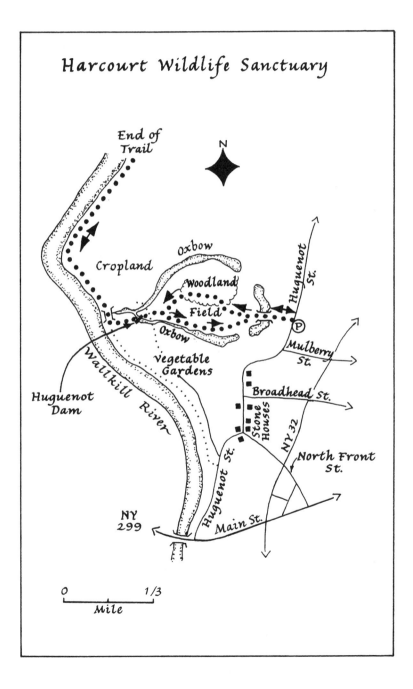

Harcourt Wildlife Sanctuary

End of Trail

N

Cropland

Oxbow

Woodland

Field

Oxbow

Huguenot St.

P

Mulberry St.

Vegetable Gardens

Broadhead St.

Wallkill River

Stone Houses

Huguenot Dam

NY 32

North Front St.

Huguenot St.

NY 299

Main St.

0   1/3
   Mile

Harcourt
Wildlife Sanctuary

Location: New Paltz
Distance: 1 mile
Owner: Huguenot Historical Society

The woods and fields along the Huguenot Path are reminiscent of the river meadows and bottomland woods of Britain and Germany. In fact, as many as half the species of trees and herbs on the site are European. Being a riverside wood, the birding throughout is superb.

Access

Huguenot Street runs parallel to the Wallkill River in the village of New Paltz. It is the last right turn when headed west on Main Street before you cross the Wallkill River bridge at the west end of town. Drive past three roads on your right, keeping on Huguenot Street as it bends. Just past the third right, Mulberry Street, there is a dirt pull-off on your right, large enough for one car, opposite the trailhead. For information, call 914-255-1660.

Trail

The Huguenot Path leads down to the oxbow lake and a view of Mohonk's Sky Top tower. Approach slowly and quietly, watching for herons and ducks. A carpet of green swirled scum coats the stagnant water. Peer closely or, better yet, scoop up in your palm some of the minute floating plants. Not scum at all, little duckweed (*Lemna* sp.) is the larger floating plant with the lobes. A thread of a white root hangs from each. The smaller ovals are watermeal *(Wolffia)*, the smallest of all flowering plants. They feel like cornmeal between the fingers. These plants constitute a major part of waterfowl diets, especially just before the autumn migration. Iridescent oil slicks the bank mud. As with the duckweed and watermeal, this is another indication of a healthy ecosystem, the natural by-product of anaerobic, or non–oxygen using, bacteria that live in the muck and help decay organic matter.

The shore grows rife in purple loosestrife *(Lythrum salicaria)*. The country does have several native purple and yellow loosestrifes, but this magenta European species has so cloaked American wetlands that folks take its flowering in late summer as part of the natural poetry of the landscape. Purple loosestrife outcompetes native cattails, sedges, and bulrushes in wetlands, but over the years it has become an important food source for cecropia and polyphemus moth caterpillars and a nesting site for the American goldfinch. In Europe the flowers were once placed across the yokes of oxen to gentle the beasts. Visit in August to see the loosestrife bloom at its peak. It is tall, up to 4 feet high, the flower spikes abuzz with bees come to make honey. The whole valley floor turns purple.

Cross the oxbow on the boardwalk. At the fork, keep straight to skirt the edge of a large successional field. Our largest local flycatcher, the kingbird, with a white band along the edge of its flared black tail, flits from perch to perch hunting insects on the wing in the old field populated by goldenrods. You will begin to pass young pin oaks. Recognize them by their deeply lobed, sharp-tipped leaves and spindly spikes of twisted lower limbs that droop from the trunk. Witch trees I call them when in their dark and leafless state. Enter an open bottomland woods of pin oak, ash, and red maple.

Anywhere along this walk it is worth trying out your spishing call. This is the sound one makes when calling a cat. "Spish, spish, spish" will attract warblers and orioles. If you are standing out in the open, you will see them flitting among the upper tree limbs giving you the look-over. Conceal yourself motionless between shrubs and they will come very close.

In spring wild greens push up through the wet, black, silty flood-soil. The royal purple blooms of violet can be plucked and tossed among your salad greens. The wild scallions commonly called onion grass can be eaten raw or added to soups (do not harvest it here, though; find some outside the sanctuary). Large-girthed pin oak

The boardwalk leads across the oxbow overrun with purple loosestrife (Lythrum salicaria). *Sky Top and Eagle Cliff of the Shawangunk are on the horizon.*

stand knee deep in verdant garlic mustard, jack-in-the-pulpit, and sensitive fern.

As you walk through a field busy with sleek, shiny grackles and robins, you view Bontecou Crag and the other Shawangunk ridges owned by Mohonk Preserve. At the intersection beneath the silver maple *(Acer saccharinum),* turn right toward the river. Whereas red maple is the maple of the Hudson and Delaware Valleys' swamps, silver maple is the waterside maple of major rivers. At the farm road, jog left and follow toward the town's vegetable plots, rented out annually to garden enthusiasts. Along this farm road crowd many European edibles and medicinals, including stinging nettle, yellow dock, the tall angelica *(Angelica atropurpurea),* and the broad-leafed burdock.

Return back the way you came to a left turn onto the Huguenot Path. Here is the Huguenot Dam, a long earthen embankment through which the path cuts. Its foundation of stones that was the gate to regulate waterflow can be seen in the water of the oxbow on your right. It has been said that the oxbow was used as a fishing weir. The dam gate was opened and the river let in, along with its fish. Once closed, the fish were trapped within the oxbow and were easier to harvest.

Arrive at the oxbow's outlet into the quiet, silty Wallkill River. *Kil* is Dutch for stream, so it is sufficient to say Wallkill. Did I say "quiet Wallkill"? The flat water belies the power flowing beneath the surface. Come during spring in a flood year when a new layer of fertile silt is washed across the valley floor.

Head over the footbridge and follow downriver through lush woods succulent with green growth. Cropland stretches out of sight on your right. In the last week of April and the first week of May, watch both sides of the path for spring-beauty *(Claytonia virginica)* and adder's-tongue *(Erythronium americanum)*. Lush poison ivy twines up the tree trunks furry red with tendrils and urushiol acid potent enough to give you a rash in midwinter. Across the ground the poison ivy grows as a ground cover. Watch for muskrats gathering fodder on the bank or swimming along the shore. At the signpost that marks the end of Huguenot Path, try out your spishing call to attract oriole, sparrows, and warblers. The local Revolutionary War militia once trained in the wide fields to your right.

Return the way you came across the footbridge. If you wish, you may continue south along the Wallkill. This will lead you to Huguenot Street, where a left turn will take you through the entire old Huguenot village and to your car. Otherwise, from the bridge retrace your steps past Huguenot Dam, jog left onto the farm road, and then right. At the fork beneath the silver maple, bear right into the field to view the rest of the oxbow lake. The trail follows the oxbow edge. At the boardwalk, turn right and up the short slope to reach your car.

A visit to New Paltz is not complete until you have walked Huguenot Street, one of the oldest streets in America; its original stone houses were built in the 1600s and 1700s. Guided tours are available. For information, call 914-255-1660.

Shawangunk Multiple Use Area

Location: Gardiner
Distance: 1 mile
Owner: State of New York

This forest in the shadow of the Trapps is popular for campers who climb the Shawangunk cliffs. The unmarked trails through moist and sunny woodland veined by brooks are easy to follow and lead to an old beaver meadow grown up in vervain.

Access

From the Wallkill River bridge as you leave New Paltz, drive 5.2 miles west on NY 299. Park on your left at the state forest sign.

Trail

Take any of several paths at the west side of the parking area past some campsites, and find the trail in the southwest corner that leads steeply downhill directly away from NY 299. Listen for the laughing-clown call of the pileated woodpecker, a resident of these deciduous woods of black birch, sugar maple, pignut and shagbark hickory, tulip-tree, and oaks.

At the bottom of the hill, turn left past more campsites. The trail parallels a brook that runs through the woods on your right. The woodland's shrub layer contains witch-hazel, ironwood, maple-leaf viburnum, black birch saplings, flowering dogwood, and, now and then, a surviving sapling of American chestnut. You will be seeing a lot of witch-hazel *(Hamamelis virginiana)* in these woods. At the trail intersection, turn right across the brook. Keep straight through the next campsite. The trail narrows and enters a thicket of black birch saplings. When young, black birch is highly shade tolerant. As it ages,

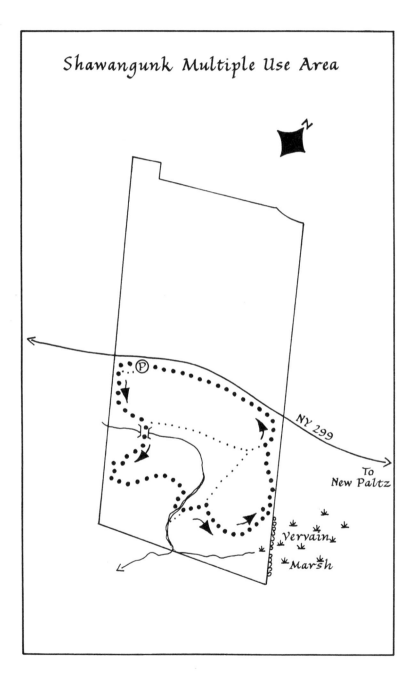

it becomes less tolerant, until upon maturity it requires full sunlight. These saplings appear to have taken advantage of the greater amount of sunlight afforded by the chopping down of a few mature trees (some time ago, by the look of the rotted stumps).

Cross a brook. Just beneath the mud lies a layer of blue-gray clay that you might expose if you slip on the bank. Walk through a grove of witch-hazel, and at the wide woods road and campsite turn right. The alley here beneath witch-hazel and black birch is a good spot to look at mushrooms brought up after a rain. At the fork, bear left. Follow until you see a bright green field on your right. Keep on and watch for a vague herd path that leads down to the beaver meadow at the dilapidated stone wall crossing the meadow.

This bright field was once woodland that reclaimed abandoned pastureland. Beaver dammed the brook and flooded the trees, killing them. Some silver-weathered trunk skeletons still stand, punctured by the nesting holes of woodpeckers. Dead, standing trees are important wildlife habitat. A New York State Department of Environmental Conservation map shows this as a beaver pond in 1985. At some point the beaver left, the dam was breached, the pond drained, and the meadow flourished in the rich pond silt. It is now a mixture of wetland and meadow species that includes grasses, sedges, cattail, phragmites rush, jewelweed, goldenrods, thistles, meadowsweet, and an incredible amount of blue vervain. There are also a few young trees, such as red maple saplings.

Although it is common, I know of only one other site in the Hudson Valley with as much blue vervain *(Verbena hastata)* in it as this beaver meadow. This plant usually occurs as at most a handful of individuals, more commonly singly here and there. There must be hundreds at this site. The vivid purple-blue flowers begin to open at the bases of their candelabra bloom-buds in July and advance in rings of blue up their candles to the tips by September. The dried seed spikes remain through the winter. Herbalists use the flowers to treat fevers, headaches, pleurisy, and ulcers.

If you bushwhack along the exceptionally dry bank edge to the stream's mouth, you will find the breached beaver dam, now little more than a longitudinal mound overgrown with plants. Beyond the

The vervain meadow and the white cliffs of the Trapps

view of the green meadow rises the white cliff of Sky Top, crowned by the stone tower at Mohonk Mountain House. Watch for damselflies flitting over the sun-shadowed water like butterflies on black wings attached to slender, peacock green bodies. These are male black-winged damselflies *(Calopteryx maculata)*. The wings of females are dark gray with a white mark called a stigma near the tips. Their dark gray bodies are only faintly iridescent. When a damselfly alights upon a leaf, twig, or stone, it folds its wings delicately over its back, whereas the close relative the dragonfly rests with its wings spread horizontally like an airplane ready to taxi.

If you cross the brook and bushwhack along the far side of the meadow, you will gain spacious views of the white Shawangunk cliffs called the Trapps and hear the technical rock climbers shouting things like, "On belay!" "Off belay!" "Rope!" "Rock!" Wear long pants to push through the smartweed, thistle, and cut-grass. State property ends at the stone wall, which you can follow straight across the wet meadow back to the bank with the trail. Watch your step. Cattails and phragmites mark standing water; goldenrods grow on dryer ground. Brush past bulrush and square-stemmed monkey-flower, being careful of your footing on the many fallen tree trunks hidden beneath the lush meadow leaves and stems. Warblers will chirp warning chirps at you if you wander near their breeding territories.

Return to the trail and at the next intersection bear right. You are back in the black birch and witch-hazel woods, but overhead the big trees are oaks and tulip-tree. The trail parallels NY 299. If you decide to cross the highway to wander the other parcel of Shawangunk Multiple Use Area, watch the forest floor just as you leave the trail for spotted wintergreen and ground cedar *(Lycopodium)*. The opposite parcel contains woodlands similar to what you have already seen along a loop that climbs steeply uphill and back down. A steep spur leads up toward the Trapps cliffs.

Otherwise, keep straight on the moss green road to the parking lot.

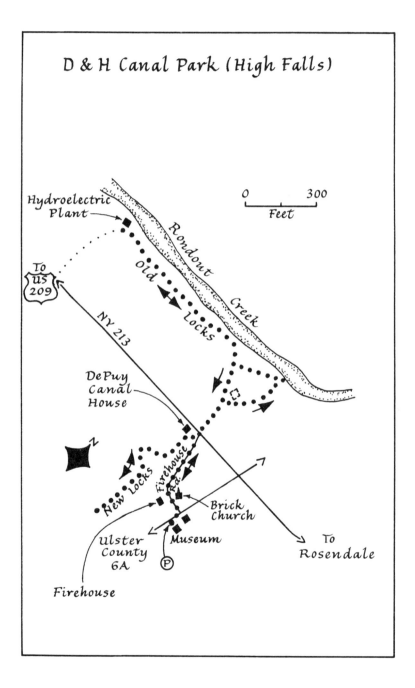

D & H Canal Park (High Falls)

Hydroelectric Plant

Rondout Creek

0   300
Feet

To US 209

Old Locks

NY 213

DePuy Canal House

New Locks

N

Firehouse Rd.

Brick Church

Ulster County 6A

Museum

P

Firehouse

To Rosendale

Delaware & Hudson
Canal Park

Location: High Falls
Distance: 1 mile
Owner: D&H Canal Historical Society
and Central Hudson

High Falls grew as one of the boom towns centered on the D&H Canal. Five locks, a railroad spur, and wagon roads that hauled millstones, timber, charcoal, cement, and various other local produce made for a busy industrial and farming center in the middle of the Rondout Valley. Most of the village is made up of intact canal-era buildings. Today those buildings are homes, businesses, and restaurants. All you need to relive the past is an imagination that removes all the trees from the site and sees past contemporary usage. This is easiest in the cooler months when the leaves are off the trees. The oldest house you will see was originally built in 1787.

The D&H Canal today is a national historic landmark. It fueled the development of much of Orange and Ulster Counties and the surrounding region, but few people today even know its name. Most of its length has been filled in. The D&H Canal Historical Society, a private, nonprofit organization, has preserved locks 16 to 20. The utility company, Central Hudson, has preserved the locks, canals, and other ruins along the Rondout where its hydroelectric plant generates electricity.

Access

The historical society's museum is located in the village of High Falls. From NY 213 turn onto Ulster County 6A and proceed 0.1 mile to parking on your left. Grounds are free and open dawn to dusk year-round. Dogs must be leashed. The museum is open May 30 through

Vickie Doyle, director of the D&H Canal Museum, points out the opposing abutment of Roebling's suspension bridge, which carried the D&H Canal—water, boats, and all—over the Rondout.

Labor Day, 11 AM–5 PM Thursday through Monday; 1–5 PM Sunday. During May, September, and October, it is open only on weekends. Admission is $2 for adults, $1 for children, $5 for families; for members it is free. For more information, call 914-687-9311.

Trail

Begin with a tour of the museum's exhibits, especially the demonstration of a working-model lock. If the museum is closed, you will find trail maps in the vestibule flanked by snubbing posts.

From the parking lot, turn right and take a look at the brick house. The millstones are made of gleaming white Shawangunk conglomerate. About 350 tons of finished millstones were shipped annually along the D&H Canal to Rosendale, where they were transferred to the Wallkill Valley Railroad for export.

Cross the street and head down Firehouse Road past the brick church and the firehouse. At Tow Path Antiques, pass by the black-topped driveway—the original towpath—and walk onto the lawn as if you are cutting over to DePuy Canal House. Before you is lock 16. Its keystone sits in the center facing the lock flanked by snubbing posts. Walk up to DePuy Canal House. At the patio take a look beneath the electric conduits on the corner of the canal house. The driven mules tramped so close that the builder purposefully beveled the structure's corner to give them room, yet that did not save the stones from deep rope cuts. Walk beside the patio and up on top of the lock.

Each of the five locks lowered boats by about 14 feet, dropping the canal over 70 feet. Lock 16 is in excellent condition. It is built of precisely cut Shawangunk conglomerate that needed no mortar. Snubbing posts and the top stone of the lock are all scarred by rope burns. I wonder how long the average mule lasted on these routes. Stories abound of the cruel treatment of orphans and the kidnapping of local children set to work driving the mules. Stories swarm thick around the memory of the D&H Canal: of rowdy saloons, brawling canawlers, prankster canawlers, canawlers who threw rocks at lock tenders or, according to historian Ann Gilcrest, used their long poles to "harass unsuspecting occupents on privies perched along the canal's berme edge"; of thieves and vandals, politicians and tourists on sightseeing trips, thousands of trudging horses and mules, laborers' riots, canal-wall breaches, accidents, floods, and washouts; of traffic jams, cholera, rival boats, drownings, hospitable grocers, and family boats. All that folklore is nearly forgotten today in towns originally grown to service the canal.

The path leads through the woods around the stonework of a canal slip. Here barges pulled out of the canal and docked to load local cement and bluestone from a railroad spur. Watch the path for glittering black bits of Pennsylvania coal. The small bridges you cross are made of Catskill bluestone. They span a waste weir, an overflow outlet also called a bypass flume. This let water bypass the locks to prevent flooding and emptied into the slip.

The private white house on the opposite side of lock 17 was the lock tender's. The backyard shed used to perch over the locking machinery. Just beyond this lock the canal widens. Originally it was lined and capped with stone. Towpaths followed both banks. Soon after this section of the canal was abandoned, in 1901, the dressed rocks began to disappear as locals pried them up and carried them off for their own building purposes. Pass locks 18 and 19. Both display what appears to be collapsing stonework but is actually open tunnels of waste weirs. The culvertlike entrance is easiest to see at the head of lock 19. Pass over a waste weir that looks like an open ditch to lock 20. Here are more snubbing posts. Return to DePuy Canal House.

To visit Central Hudson's Canal Park, cross NY 213 and walk into the driveway of the lock tender's cottage, a white house with green shutters. Walk around the picket fence and take your first right into the woods on a dirt path. You are walking the towpath beside two canals. On your right the old D&H, which opened commercially in 1828, runs beside you still lined with its original, irregularly cut stone. Just above the highest land you see is the newer D&H Canal, expanded in 1852 to accommodate wider and heavier coal barges. Along the canal route as a whole the newer canal simply replaced the older, but here in High Falls they are separate for a short distance. They joined just ahead. On your left is the foundation of a cement mill.

The canals joined at the point where you come to Rondout Creek. Stand atop the buttresses of John A. Roebling's aqueduct, sister to the suspension bridge at the D&H Canal Park in Cuddebackville. Both were marvels in their day, designed and constructed by the architect who went on to design the Brooklyn Bridge, a wonder of the world. Find the huge iron pins that secured the suspension cables. A towpath with a railing crossed beside the aerial canal.

Retrace your steps for a few yards and bear right to head up-stream. In winter there is a good view here of the natural, glacial-age falls for which the town is named. At the paved path, turn right past remains of mill races along the Rondout bank. At the wire fence with the big "NO" sign, keep straight on through—the "no" is just a list of rules for usage. This brings you to the hydroelectric plant. There are excellent interpretive signs on history and geology. Feel free to relax or picnic on the flat rocks at the water's edge. Walk up the paved path to see the upper falls and the ruins of the Norton Cement Company mill. Return back along the paved walkway to the lock tender's cottage and through the village to the museum.

John Burroughs Sanctuary

Location: West Park
Distance: 1½ miles
Owner: The John Burroughs Association

A t first breath it is somewhat daunting to describe a nature walk through the personal woods of one of America's popular nature essayists. John Burroughs Sanctuary contains the famous cabin Slabsides, one of Burroughs's refuges from ordinary busy life. Built in 1895, Slabsides is a registered national historic landmark. Burroughs loved entertaining visitors here, from presidents to day groups of college women from Vassar. He lived here for days, weeks, or whole seasons from 1873 until 1920. Upon his death in 1921, Slabsides, with 9 acres, was given to the John Burroughs Association. In 1964 and 1965, the adjoining woods were threatened with logging and development. Those additional acres were procured, bringing the sanctuary total to 170 acres.

This "secluded nook" of a sanctuary is a place for observations of natural history and strolls of philosophy. There are no sweeping views, but Burroughs preferred it that way; as he explained, "Scenery may be too fine or too grand and imposing for one's daily and hourly view." There is a safe and enclosed feeling here, yet the place lies a scant half mile from the noisy civilization that so distressed Burroughs. "Blessed Slabsides," he wrote, "the dwelling-place of peace and quiet, and such sweet thought as come to me every moment, like the breath of clover from out June meadows, and refresh and quicken my spirit."

Access

From the post office on US 9W in the hamlet of West Park, turn west onto Floyd Ackert Road. Drive 0.9 mile, through the stop sign and across the railroad tracks (the defunct station where Burroughs met

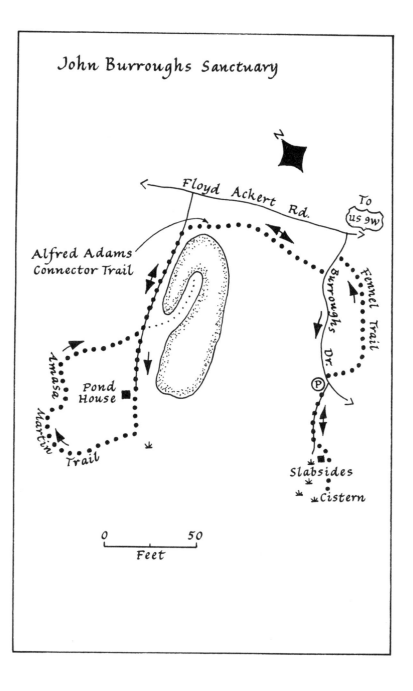

John Burroughs Sanctuary

Floyd Ackert Rd.

To US 9W

Alfred Adams
Connector Trail

Burroughs Dr.

Fennel Trail

Amasa Martin Trail

Pond House

P

Slabsides

Cistern

0   50
Feet

his guests and walked them up the path over the ridge to Slabsides), to a left on narrow Burroughs Drive. Motor up the hill 0.35 mile to Slabsides parking on the right. As the sign cautions, do not block the gate.

The preserve is always open. Slabsides is open the third Saturday in May and the first Saturday in October, 11 AM–4 PM.

Trail

Walk the driveway on pilgrimage to Slabsides through thick and dark hemlock woods mixed with white pine and deciduous trees. At the fork at the privy, bear left past low swales of spicebush. A two-story log cabin, Slabsides stands on a stone foundation on a dry ledge surrounded by a narrow band of red maple and fern swamp accompanied by spicebush, winterberry, and witch-hazel. Although Burroughs and contemporaries termed it a "rude house" and a "rustic cabin," I find Slabsides to be a fancy and grand cabin in keeping with Victorian big camp and hunting lodge romanticism, with lots of room, *two* stories, a wide porch, and a big fireplace where gentlemen like John Muir, Thomas Edison, Teddy Roosevelt, Harvey Firestone, and Henry Ford had room to stretch their legs while they philosophized and smoked cigars.

The trail to the spring passes through a corridor of spicebush *(Lindera benzoin)* and ends at a cistern sunk into the water table. If in use, it would be cleaned out and the water sparkling and deep. Burroughs claimed his health improved when he drank this water every day.

Do not climb the stone stairs, which are on private property. Return to the cabin and then to your car, but don't get in it. Walk across the road, turn left for a short distance, and on the other side of the road find the William G. Fennel Memorial Trail. Before you leave the pavement, though, look at the huge coltsfoot leaves on the verge. The second bloom of spring, yellow, dandelionlike tops seemingly pop out of nowhere with only 2 warm days' notice in early March. A European healing herb, coltsfoot was practically a required simple for the *physick* garden. In America it soon escaped and naturalized itself, much to the appreciation of Native herbalists.

Take the trail. At the top of the hemlock rise encounter the noise of traffic and neighboring homes that up until now were blocked by the ridge. The feeling of isolation evaporates. Burroughs commented on this himself, writing how the ridge "shut off . . . the vain and noisy world of railroads, steamboats, and yachts." In Burroughs's day you could see the Shawangunk and Catskills from on top of this ridge. Now it is all grown over with forest. Switchback down the steep slope. The trail leads through a cleft in the long rocky ridge, taking you gradually downhill. It is beautiful here in a silent snowfall.

Turn left at the paved road. Just uphill is your car, but if you want to keep walking you can visit the lake parcel of the preserve. On the S-curve on your right, find the Alfred Adams Connector Trail. Head down a small ridge. At the moist bottom on both sides of the path grows a shrub or small tree with paired thorns and seven hairy leaflets with smooth margins. This is northern prickly ash *(Xanthoxylum americanum),* whose leaves were once chewed to alleviate toothache. Like spicebush, the torn leaf smells lemony.

At the dirt road, turn left. Soon you arrive at the sanctuary pond. In autumn, come on a bright day to see the reds, yellows, purples, oranges, and bronzes reflected in the water and the flaming red maples contrasted against the deep green hemlocks and the deep blue sky. Perhaps the most striking foliage, though, is of the poison ivy straggling up the posts and elm trees beside the road. Its yellow is intense, accompanied by soft orange, pink, and peach.

Pass a mix of many of the region's lowland tree and shrub species, around the pond mixed deciduous, on its rock island the addition of white pine and hemlock. You will see red and sugar maple, chestnut, red and white oak, sycamore, elm, basswood, black birch, sassafras, witch-hazel, mountain laurel, hickory, white ash, ironwood, winterberry, beech, maple-leaf viburnum, and flowering dogwood. At the end of the drive are an old hotel site's stone walls and foundations. In the center grows a giant elm with the classic, multibranched, sweeping vase shape that made it famous as a city street shade ornamental.

At Pond House, keep straight along the pond on the Amasa Martin Trail. This leads through gentle woods excellent for quiet

The retreat cabin "Slabsides." The writings of John Burroughs fueled a bonfire of nature appreciation and interest in preservation at a time when the eastern United States was being clear-cut, the white-tailed deer eliminated, and the passenger pigeon about to become extinct.

nature study. It loops through a sugar maple and white ash woodland grown up in garlic mustard, past woodland pools, to a marsh overlook of Black Creek. The trail is faintly marked, the signs worn, so keep a sharp lookout. Listen for the hooting of great horned owl and the madcap clown-laughter of pileated woodpecker. The woodland on the return side of the loop passes into a cooler climate of mixed deciduous trees embedded with pockets of hemlock and the black water of woodland pools. Once back at Pond House, return the way you came, turning right onto Burroughs Drive to find your car.

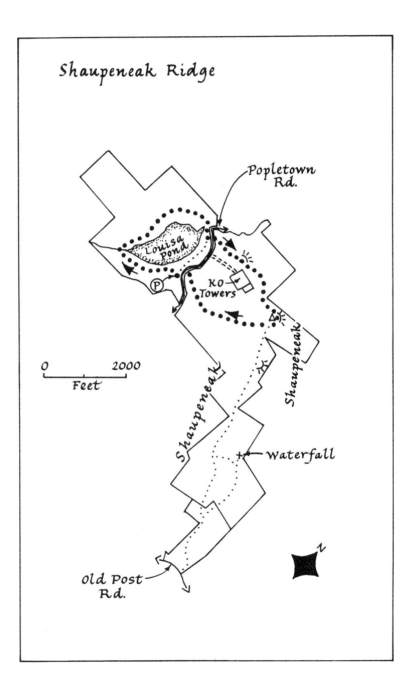

Shaupeneak Ridge

Popletown Rd.

Louisa Pond

KO Towers

P

0   2000
      Feet

Shaupeneak

Shaupeneak

Waterfall

Old Post Rd.

Shaupeneak Ridge

Location: Esopus
Distance: 2 miles
Owner: Scenic Hudson

The highest of the Marlboro Hills, Shaupeneak and nearby Hussy's or Huzzy's Hill to the north make up the end of a row of precipitous forested ridges that shadow the Hudson River trough between Marlboro and Kingston. Scenic Hudson was concerned with protecting the viewshed of these hills from the Hudson River and its eastern shore. Its purchase of almost 500 acres on Shaupeneak has opened to the public Louisa Pond, perhaps the richest wildlife habitat in this book's collection of sites. The pond is mostly a place of pond insects and other invertebrates, fish, reptiles, amphibians, and birds, but there are also many mammals. The marsh is a botanizer's paradise, and the birding is superb. The ridge, a cooperative recreation area, is managed jointly by Scenic Hudson, New York State's Department of Environmental Conservation, and the West Esopus Landowners Association, an impressive example of conservation partnership.

Nicholas Shoumatoff's research among Lenape speakers reveals that Shaupeneak is derived from a word in the Unami dialect, *shohpeneok,* which translates as "people of the shore."

Access

From the stoplight in Port Ewan, motor south on US 9W for about 6 miles. Turn right onto Old Post Road/Ulster County 16. Go 0.7 mile, crossing the railroad tracks, passing the lower trailhead of Shaupeneak, and climb. In 0.7 mile, Old Post Road turns right. Be careful not to continue straight here onto Swartekill Road. Just before this intersection you pass Poppletown House on your left, a historic Dutch stone farmhouse. Continue on Old Post Road for another 1.2 miles as it winds up the ridge. Keep straight onto Popletown Road,

White water lily and pickerelweed on still Louisa Pond early in the morning

marked with a dead-end sign. Go 0.8 mile to parking on your left. The preserve is open dawn to dusk. Dogs are allowed. The property is open to hunting during deer and turkey seasons. For more information, call the Scenic Hudson main office in Poughkeepsie, 914-473-4440.

Trail

A combination of open water, marsh, and floating bog at Louisa Pond heightens its suitability to wildlife. Diversity increases a land's carrying capacity. Herons, ducks, geese, hawks, owls, reams of passerines, and other birds use this wetland on a regular or a seasonal basis. It is ideally located along the Hudson Valley flypath, one of North America's major migration routes, on top of a secluded mountain on an uninhabited stretch of backcountry road. This is a place where wildlife can flourish with little disturbance from human activity. The dead trees indicate the water level was once higher, probably from beaver building on top of the human-made dam. The dam flooded a natural basin carved out by the Wisconsin glacier. The weathered, standing trees are invaluable resting and hunting perches for owls, hawks, and kingfisher, and also make good nesting sites for wood-peckers and wood duck.

If you want to see birds and mammals in summer, the best time of day to visit is in early morning, no later than 8 AM. Deer and birds are crepuscular, which means they are most active at dawn and dusk. On my first visit here I saw an osprey and a full-grown juvenile great horned owl, which sat on a dead tree limb overlooking the water for half an hour making the baby sound that lets its parents know where it is. Once the sun is up and beaming, most larger animals take to cover for the day.

For the water creatures, the time of day sometimes makes no difference. Sit by the pond edge and watch the show. You might see the huge dark shell of a snapping turtle grazing among the submerged aquatic vegetation, or flush a large pike from the shallows, or a family of wood ducks. Dragonflies hover over emergent woody and herbaceous marsh flora too numerous to list here. Salamanders and water insects go about life in the shallows. The more you look, the more you see.

The footpath carries you on top of the bank around the lake mostly under hemlocks, now and then through mixed deciduous woods of chestnut, red, and white oak, sugar maple, hickory, and black birch. Only once do you dip near the shore to cross the stone and earthen dam at the outlet; otherwise the trail keeps you away from the water's edge. The open water is ringed with pickerelweed, arrowhead, spatterdock, and white water lily. Old beaver lodges and dams can be found in the cattail and woody marsh. The only mar on the view is the communications towers on top of Shaupeneak.

The land was farmed in the past and more recently timbered, but you'd never know it except for the periodic rot-blackened sawn stumps and the overgrown skidder paths that the trail follows in places. Here you might find dense growths of white snakeroot *(Eupatorium rugosum)*. Many medicinals have been confounded under the English name, but all were used as antidotes to reptile bites and insect stings, and the *Eupatoria* are famous fever remedies.

As you parallel Popletown Road, watch for the left turn that will lead to Shaupeneak's crest. Cross the paved road and make your way through the sugar maple and oak woods with some hop horn-beam and pignut hickory and patches of hemlock. The trail angles up steeply along the ridge slope and up and over knolls. Soon you gain seasonal views of the Catskills through the trees. At first the woods seem homogenous, but then you encounter a rich mosaic of four basic habitats.

Blowdowns have allowed full sunlight to reach the forest floor. In these places thickets of moosewood compete with other species for the new light. These provide wildlife cover and tender woody stems and buds for food. Large, rotting, sawn stumps of cut timber indicate older openings, which are now populated by young trees and hidden by hay-scented fern. Mature hardwood stands and older hemlock groves remain from the "original" forest that reclaimed the mountain from pasture. Bedrock basins form wetland pockets and seasonal wood-land pools. This diversity makes Shaupeneak extremely valuable to animals for food, protective cover, and reproductive sites.

Hemlocks coat the north-facing steep slope of the mountain all the way to the sedge-floored ridgetop crest, so the view at the summit is obscured. When the leaves are down on the deciduous trees, there are eastern views of the Hudson River and Dutchess County. The trail splits. The left fork heads down the steep slope to a knob with more seasonal views and then downhill all the way to Old Post Road. A side spur off that leads to a waterfall. The right fork leads downhill back toward your car, up and over knolls and onto an old woods road for the descent. At the foot of the slope in an old pasture this road turns left, but your trail keeps straight for the parking area on Pople-town Road.

Esopus Meadows Point

Location: Port Ewen
Distance: 1¼ miles
Owner: Scenic Hudson

This 68-acre preserve contains sills of shale bedrock and troughs of wetland, making for a diversified woodland. Esopus Meadows Point has been a historical riverside landmark since the days when, fairylike, it is said the meadows appeared at low tide and the cows were sent out to graze on the grasses. Most likely those cows were wading out to chomp on wild celery, a native aquatic plant. Nowadays they would find mostly mouthfuls of Eurasian water milfoil and the hated European and Asian water chestnuts whose fierce-pronged caltrops would poke their tongues.

The meadows are actually tidal shallows where the Hudson runs 1 to 3 feet deep clear out to the lighthouse that marks the shipping channel. Under the growing heat of the summer sun, you can see the clogging "meadow" around the clock. In winter come to see the ice floes, broken by the cutter ships, whispering as they slither and bump one against another.

Access

From the stoplight in Port Ewen, drive south on US 9W 0.5 mile to a left on narrow River Road. Wind along for 2.7 miles to parking on your left at the Esopus Meadows Environmental Center. The preserve is open dawn to dusk. Dogs are allowed. For more information, call the Scenic Hudson offices in Poughkeepsie, 914-473-4440.

Trail

To the right of the environmental center along the driveway, pick up the blue-marked trail over the Klyne Esopus Kill (a muddy little

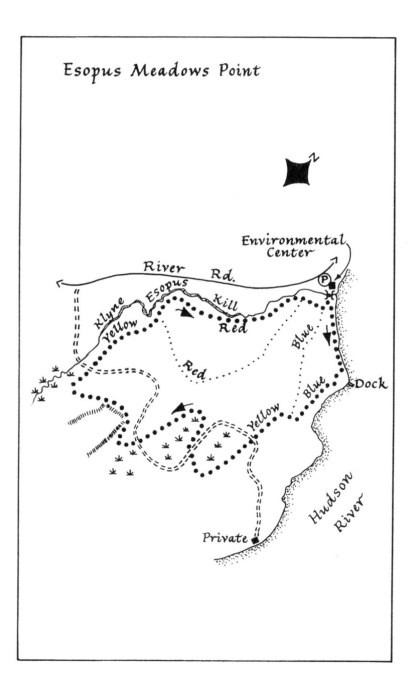

Esopus Meadows Point

brook that you will be seeing much more of later) and follow along the Hudson River shore. Whenever you walk directly beside the Hudson's graveled beach, you can count on seeing dull-leaf indigo bush *(Amorpha fruticosa)*, and here it is. Sprays of deep indigo flowers bloom in June glowing with orange anthers of golden pollen.

At low tide you can leave the trail to walk the beach. In summer the algae bloom leaves behind a smelly green mat. In winter there is ice. In all seasons there are the black caltrops of the water chestnut *(Trapa natans)*, sharp enough to puncture a sneaker's sole. Kids call them devil heads. These and other plants like them inspired the weapon of war that is scattered on the field before advancing cavalry or tires: an iron ball with four spikes so apportioned that no matter how the caltrop falls, one disabling spike sticks upright. Crack one of these seed pods open to find the edible white meat, unrelated to the savory spikerush tuber of Oriental cuisine. These nuts remain viable for 12 years and are cultivated in Asia for food.

Erik Kiviat, of Hudsonia, reports that water chestnut outcompetes native and even other introduced water plants, and speeds eutrophication, or filling in, of bays and shallows. It is impossible to boat, swim, or fish in such a tangle of growth. Insects living on the floating rosettes, however, provide a "restaurant" for birds. Esopus Meadows used to be an important resting and feeding stop for migrating waterfowl and an invaluable spawning ground and nursery for fish. The shift from water celery to water chestnut may be changing this.

The woods road ends at a dock where you have a view of the great green expanse of choking water chestnut seeming to extend clear to Esopus Meadows Lighthouse. Efforts are under way to restore this structure, which was one of the last manned lighthouses on the Hudson. (Phone the Hudson River Maritime Museum at 914-338-0071 for further information.) Built in 1839 and rebuilt in 1872, it was one of nine Hudson River "family stations" under the jurisdiction of the US Lighthouse Service. The various keepers and their families cleaned and tended the lens, living for years in isolation out on the water in the white clapboard house built on a granite pier. Their logs report several large barges jammed against the house in storms. One

In a boat you can get close enough to the Esopus Meadows Lighthouse to see that the "windows" are actually paintings on wood nailed over the real windows. Each "window" has a different painting.

winter, great ice sheets dislodged the structure from its foundation. Keeper John Kerr lived in the lighthouse with his wife, two pet skunks, a bantam rooster, and a dog. In 1939, the lighthouse came under the control of the US Coast Guard. In 1965, Esopus Meadows Lighthouse was closed and automated.

The river bottom drops 50 to 100 feet at the lighthouse. Nearly all the Hudson River's shortnose sturgeon spend their winters in this narrow channel beside Esopus Point. Come spring, they swim north to Troy to spawn. Across the river on the east bank spread the green lawns and marble façades of older river estates. Some, like Mills Mansion and Wilderstein, are open to the public (see *Walks and Rambles in Dutchess and Putnam Counties*).

From the dock, backtrack to the blue-marked trail into the woods up onto the bluff. Sugar maple grows on the slope, but the dryer blufftop is the abode of red oak and white pine. Mounds of shale mark historic, small-scale quarries for road-building and other local usage. The trail bends away from the river. Watch for the blue markers that lead left through woods of sugar maple, red and chestnut oak, hop hornbeam, and hickory. At the intersection, turn left onto the yellow-marked trail. By now you have seen how the landform is based on the geology of parallel north- to south-running shale sills. The troughs in between collect and hold water. Cross the private driveway. Please do not walk along this dirt road; keep to the trail. The path leads along the xeric, or extremely dry, bedrock sill around a strip of wetland at its foot. The troughs between the xeric shale sills collect and hold water, supporting swamp or woodland pools, and enclaves of red maple and swamp azalea. Some are overgrown by cat briar. Such close juxtaposition of different habitats is valuable for wildlife. Many animals require more than one habitat to complete their life cycles. Also, diversity of habitats supports a greater diversity of species.

Come down off the sill, across the foot of the swamp, and up the next sill. Cross the driveway into a xeric upland of stunted oaks and hickories. Ebony spleenwort ferns *(Asplenium platyneuron)* rooted in crevices indicate calcareous, alkaline conditions in the bedrock.

Cross the drive once more for another shale sill and a trough wetland. When you come off this last sill, you enter a tall woodland of sugar maple, black birch, and red and white oak. Stone walls indicate that this level land was once used for farming. These tall trees are probably the same age as those on top of the xeric sills. The differences in height and girth are due to the availability of water. Be certain to sight from marker to marker here, as there are old trails that lead in several directions other than the yellow path. Follow until you reach the bluff of the silty Klyne Esopus Kill. This flooded area was caused by the driveway culvert. The nutrient-rich muck is grown up in greenery smothered beneath the gold, threadlike stems of the parasitic dodder.

Cross the driveway for the last time as you follow the brook blufftop. Pass large-girthed locust, white and red oak, and sugar maple interspersed in the woodland. The unpretentious Klyne Esopus Kill has eroded a magnificent ravine. *Klyne* is Dutch for "little" and *kil* means "creek." The wall's moist, cool microclimate supports hemlock and Christmas fern. The yellow trail runs into the red-marked trail. Keep straight along the ravine's rim.

The trail crosses the woodland and passes a farmer's rock pile. Witch-hazel shades the path as you parallel the Kill. At the blue trail turn left, and left again at the Hudson River.

Ulster Landing Park

Location: Ulster and Saugerties
Distance: 3½ miles
Owner: County of Ulster

The trails of 100-acre Ulster Landing Park traverse riverside woodland, a cedar grove, and small hemlock gorges. What makes the place exceptional is 3000 feet of Hudson River shoreline. In addition to that, Scenic Hudson property continues north to the abandoned Coast Guard station at Turkey Point. These properties combined create an unparalleled sandy stretch of public-access beach traversable only at low tide. The Coast Guard owns Turkey Point and its derelict bulkhead. This property is closed to the public. A couple hundred feet west of the federal property is the 48 acres of Turkey Point forest owned by the State of New York and managed by the Department of Environmental Conservation. This is open to the public.

Access

From the intersection of NY 199 and NY 32 at the Kingston-Rhinecliff Bridge, take NY 32 north for 1.5 miles to a right on Ulster Landing Road toward the Hudson River. Travel 2.3 miles to the county park entrance on the right. Park at the swimming beach. Ulster Landing Park is generally open Memorial Day through Labor Day, 10 AM to 8 PM; however, each year opening and closing dates and hours may vary slightly. For information, call 914-331-0186, ext. 245; or 914-336-8484. There is a locked gate when the park is closed. The daily entrance fee is $1.50 for adults and $1 for children. Before or after your walk, you can also swim in the river on a sand beach attended by a lifeguard, enjoy a picnic, launch your boat, Jet-Ski, and hold parties with a permit. Dogs are allowed on leash only.

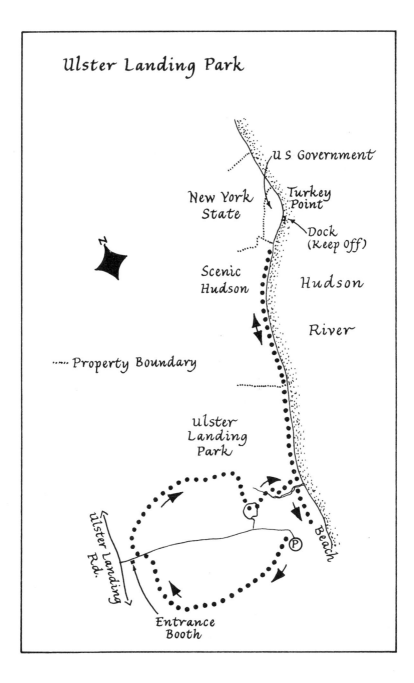

Ulster Landing Park

Trail

Check the daily weather almanac in your local newspaper to time this walk for low tide. Before heading out on the trail, you might want to stroll the beach southward beneath the huge cottonwood trees toward the boat launch. The Kingston-Rhinecliff Bridge stands downstream, Tivoli South Bay is across the water, and Cruger Island is upriver as the Hudson curves behind its western bank. The greenish estuary water washes the shore, bringing in black, spiny, hard caltrops from the Eurasian water chestnut that grows underwater in the shallows. Don't step on one of these seed cases with bare feet! It is a good idea to walk the beach with sandals or sneakers, but still be careful not to tread on them. Broken red bricks also litter the beach, along with silver-weathered driftwood and long, green "seaweed" leaves of wild celery, a valuable food plant for wildfowl. Two brickyards once flanked Ulster Landing Park and dumped thousands of bricks offshore. Tides, storms, and ship wakes heave up the bricks. Park staff are forever cleaning them off the beach.

From the parking lot walk back up the entrance road until you stand directly opposite the swimming section of the beach. Turn left into the woods on the white-marked trail. Follow upstream alongside a brook ravine. Cross the tiny brook that cut the wide ravine and follow through a stand of black locust trees. The white trail takes a right-hand turn and meanders through red maple, black cherry, and hickory woods. At a tiny brook crossing, feel the soil. It is sticky with that same clay that attracted so many brickworks to the banks of the Hudson River in bygone years.

The forest floor opens up as the trail angles along a brook bank. This is a good place to watch up ahead for turkey. Extremely wary birds, they will probably see you before you see them and make off silently between the tree trunks. Cross the brook on stones. At the yellow-marked trail keep straight, following the white trail, which will emerge from the woods onto the paved entrance road. Walk left toward the ticket booth. To the left of the booth is a brown house. Walk behind that house along its driveway about 50 feet, where the white trail resumes on your left.

The trail leads over a patch of crest woodland, then steadily downhill into a plantation of planted red pines and a grove of red cedar. These cedars, also called junipers, are old and stand tall; they are doomed, however. See how the lower limbs are all dead and only the crowns are alive with needles? Red cedar requires full sunlight. They probably sprouted when this was an open field. Junipers can neither grow nor reproduce in their own shade. But young, shade-tolerant red maples and white pines can, and they have overtopped the cedars and taken their sunlight. This natural reforestation process, called succession, is a common sight in the Hudson Valley where agriculture has declined.

At the parking lot, turn left to follow the wood's edge to where the white trail reenters the woods at a huge oak tree. The remnant stubs of horizontal limbs on this oak indicate that in the past it grew all alone in an open field. The trail leads downhill. Pass the blue-marked trail and cross the stream on sills of rock at the head of a gorge.

The trail leads steeply downhill through hemlocks along the gorge lip. Please keep on the path. It is well designed to take you to several vantage points to view the waterfalls (these may dry up come summer), while lessening impact on this fragile environment. Hemlocks are susceptible to compaction around their roots, and gorge edges are prone to erosion and collapse. If you have young children with you, hold them by the hand. Polypody fern coats the rocks, and moosewood grows in the cool ravine.

At the bottom, turn right and leave the trail to follow the brook out to the Hudson River. It seems like the ocean here. Actually, in many ways this *is* the ocean, an "arm of the sea." The light shines brightly, the river wind blows, and the low tide reveals a rippled sandbar. This section of the Hudson is an estuary, not a river. The glacial gorge of the Hudson riverbed lies at sea level for 152 upstream miles. Salt water does not reach north farther than Poughkeepsie due to the Hudson's tremendous freshwater flow, yet the ocean tides rise and fall clear north to the dam at Troy.

Turn left to wander upriver (or, more properly, upestuary). This beach is an excellent place for botanizing riverside flora. Find water plantain *(Alisma plantago-aquatica,* formerly *triviale),* the famous medicinals boneset *(Eupatorium perfoliatum)* and Joe-Pye weed

(E. purpureum), fringed loosestrife *(Lysimachia ciliata),* ashleaf maple *(Acer negundo),* silver maple *(A. saccharinum),* and dull-leaf indigo bush *(Amorpha fruticosa).* One of the most interesting is the long, thin, green, grasslike plant growing in the water that makes the shoreline resemble a tidal saltwater marsh. This is a bulrush sedge, called chairmaker's rush *(Scirpus americanus).*

You can see Turkey Point in the distance, marked by a green coastal navigation light. Splash through the shallows, rest on the white sand. Find freshwater mussel shells. Walk the sandbar. Do not swim here out of sight of a lifeguard, and especially never off the deepwater Coast Guard dock. The Hudson may look like a lake, but the main current rips right past here and will carry you away faster than you may be able to swim.

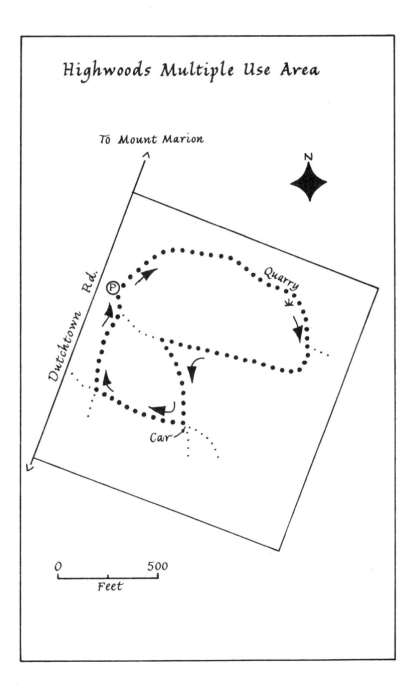

Highwoods Multiple Use Area

Highwoods
Multiple Use Area

Location: Saugerties
Distance: ¾ mile
Owner: State of New York

T his 43-acre state forest is a pleasant site to visit for a quiet walk in the woods and for nature study, especially with children. The many wide woods roads are unmarked, so you need to be careful to keep a sense of direction. Some of the many side roads lead to nothing more than hunters' campsites. Not all of these roads are shown on the map.

Access

From the intersection of NY 199, US 209, and US 9W just north of Kingston, take US 9W north for 4.5 miles to Glenerie. Turn west (left) onto Ulster County 32/Glasco Turnpike. Go 3.2 miles to a left onto Dutchtown Road. Proceed 1.1 miles to a parking lot on your left.

Trail

Facing away from Dutchtown Road, take the old road on your left into the woods, a mixture of hemlock, sugar maple, hickory, oak, moosewood, and white pine with a few hop hornbeam. Throughout this preserve you will keep on the main road, bypassing all side roads. In some places trees have fallen and let in the sunlight. The trail corridor is itself a clearing of the forest canopy that allows full sunlight to penetrate to the forest floor. White pine seedlings are proliferating in all of these openings, but none can be found in the shade. White pine requires full sunlight to the extent that seedlings cannot grow beneath their parent's shade. Instead, they commonly colonize full sunlit fields. White pine's long leaves are attached to the stem in bundles of five needles, making it easy to remember (five

An inviting old woods road

letters making up the word "white"). The name actually derives from the white sap that frosts the cones and dribbles from wounds in the bark. Some of the canopy openings have sprouted up moosewood, or striped maple *(Acer pensylvanicum)*.

The trail bed is a good place for nature study. Dwarf cinquefoil *(Poentilla canadensis)* and path rush *(Juncus tenuis)* are highly tolerant of trampling and typically found growing on or along the margins of well-used woods roads. "Cinquefoil" is a corruption of the French *cinque feuilles,* "five leaves." Each leaf is made up of five leaflets on a creeping, hairy stalk that bears yellow flowers. The entire plant is reminiscent of the three-leaved strawberry. Its larger cousin, common cinquefoil, is also sometimes confused with it. The short, wiry, gold-green foliage of path rush actually seems to improve with trampling. At first glance, this import from Europe and North Africa looks like a grass. Another name for it is wire grass. It brushes the ankles of the walker and sprinkles the socks with seeds.

Examine the many ferns and mosses that grow on the trail. Mosses begin as tiny spores borne on the wind to a fertile and moist spot. Each spore swells and grows into a mass of green threads that send up leafy stalks—what we commonly recognize as the plant called moss. The stalks are usually either male or female, with both sexes growing side by side. One rainy night or dewy morning, sperm from the males swims along the film of water down the male plant, up the female plant, and into her to fertilize her egg. The egg then grows a stalk, on top of which ripens a spore-bearing capsule. It is fun to open these when they are fully formed. An outer, papery sheath slips off like a slipper to reveal a chamber capped with a round door. When ripe, this fitted door simply falls open to spill out the spores upon the wind.

A recent rain will bring up mushrooms among the mosses. One easy to recognize is *Russula,* with its red top and white gills beneath. Mushrooms are important decomposers that recycle nutrients from dying plants and animals back into the ecosystem. Old, rotting stumps of trees cut for timber provide nutrition for lichens. Search for the red-capped British soldier lichen, or the green horns of fairy cup.

Soon you arrive at a pool of water on your right. Dragonflies perch on bulrushes and false nettles. It may not look like much, but pools such as this are essential breeding sites for amphibians.

Bluestone tailings from a quarry were dumped on the left side of the trail. Since they are exposed to full sunlight for a great part of the day and provide well-drained habitat, two plants common to dry, rocky woods grow on this little island in the midst of the shaded, wetter area. Bottlebrush grass *(Elymus hystrix)* stands about 3 feet tall. The seeds on the nodding stalk head stick out perpendicular from the stem like its namesake. *Carex arctata* looks at first glance like long, reclining grass. Feel the dry, edged stems. This is the most common sedge of open woods in the Hudson Valley, blooming in the spring.

As you continue along the trail, exploring if you wish the quarry on the left, the ground elevates slightly and soil drainage improves. *Carex arctata* and grasses replace the wet-loving ferns, moosewood disappears, chestnut oak increases in frequency, and lowbush blueberry appears. These are all indications of dryer habitat. Bear right at the fork past small bedrock outcrops on your right. Compare this weathered bluestone to the fresher quarry cuts. It is difficult to see that they are the same rock. Rain, wind, snow, and temperature changes slowly wear Hudson Valley rocks to a uniform gray and encase them within a weathered cortex. This shell must be removed to expose the rock's true color and sparkle. This is why rock hounds carry rock hammers; to identify a rock you have to break it open so you can see it. And when you do, the glittering minerals can take your breath away. Rocks exposed to weather also get colonized by life. These bedrock outcrops are coated in gray, green, and white crustose (crustlike) and foliose (leaflike) lichens. Mosses, ferns, and herbs sprout from soil-filled crevices. Such soil gathering is a miniature version of the same process seen in the Shawangunks and the Hudson Highlands, where soil fills deep crevices, traps moisture, and sprouts trees.

The trail curves right and descends very slightly in elevation back into the moister woods of ferns, moosewood, and hemlock. The trail becomes somewhat obscure as it passes through a thick, dark growth of hemlock that blocks so much sunlight (up to 80 percent) and perpetuates such acidic soil that there is no undergrowth.

Turn right at the T-intersection. Keep on the main road or, if you like, explore any of the many side roads good for botanizing and peace and quiet. At the next main intersection, turn left. This will lead you to a white Mercury Monarch junked years ago. Make a sharp right onto what was once the drivable road the Monarch last traveled into hemlock woods with patches of deciduous trees. As you approach Dutchtown Road you will come to a four-way intersection. Turn right and then left for the parking lot.

Ruth Reynolds Glunt Nature Preserve

Location: Saugerties Lighthouse
Distance: 1 mile
Owner: US Coast Guard, leased to
Saugerties Lighthouse Conservancy

Saugerties has the only lighthouse on the Hudson River accessible from land. Fill begun in 1887 and finished sometime in the 1890s created the dike that connects the lighthouse to the mainland at the mouth of Esopus Creek. Here, the half-mile nature trail through 17-acre Ruth Reynolds Glunt Nature Preserve traverses a site rich in flora and history, capped by the lighthouse itself and its expansive, breezy view of the Hudson River. The naturalist can easily spend an entire afternoon bird-watching and botanizing. The historical use of the area spans centuries of storytelling: Esopus Indians, the Lighthouse Service, Hudson River anglers, ice cutting, Catskill bluestone, tides, storms, wrecks, steamships, ferries, and much more.

If you have been suffering through one of those unbearably humid and hot Hudson Valley summers, then come to the river breezes at Saugerties Lighthouse. When the sun shines, there is a bright, ocean-beach quality to the light and a nautical flavor to the white curtains blowing against the white bedroom walls of the lighthouse. It is refreshing and reminds me of how fortunate we are in the Hudson Valley to enjoy not only mountains and forests, but the sealike river, too.

Access

From the traffic light in Saugerties at the intersection of NY 32 and US 9W at Partition and Main Streets, go 0.4 mile north on US 9W to a right turn onto Mynderse Street. Go 0.4 mile to a left on Lighthouse

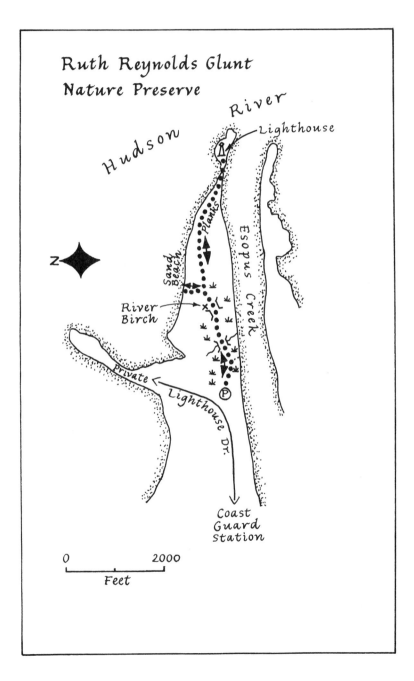

Drive. Follow for 0.7 mile to just past the Coast Guard station. Park at the trailhead lot on your right.

The trail is open any time, but the lighthouse is only open Saturday, Sunday, and holidays 2–5 PM or by appointment; call 914-246-9170 or 246-4380. Admission to the lighthouse is $3 for adults, $1 for children under 12, and free for children under 3.

Parts of the trail are submerged beneath a few inches of water at higher tides. Some people don't mind this, especially on a hot summer's day, but if you want to keep your feet dry, time your walk for low tide. High and low tides are listed under the weather almanac section of your local newspaper.

Trail

Walk through the metal fence on the lighthouse trail. Just inside the gate on your left stand a pair of huge cottonwoods that shimmer with the slightest breeze. The trail takes you through a moist and swampy woodland. Cross two footbridges. At the fork, bear left past a stand of stinging nettles amid ashleaf maples. This side trail leads to the river's edge at a cove and sand beach.

Return the way you came and at the stinging nettles turn left to continue toward the lighthouse. Wooden planks lead you through marsh flora and then back onto sand. The riverside woods are nearly pure black willow, with only a few elm and red maple. Up ahead you glimpse the lighthouse. Just as you step off the boardwalk, look on your left for one river birch *(Betula nigra).* Rare, you passed others by the Coast Guard station (watch for them on your return).

Leave the trees for a wet meadow of sweet flag or calamus, Joe-Pye weed, sedges, purple loosestrife, yellow iris, phragmites reed, narrowleaf cattail, aster, big bur reed, and dock. Over all tangle the orange stems of the parasitic dodder and the dance of pollinating butterflies.

This may be the oldest family lighthouse on the Hudson, built in 1869, but it had replaced an even older lighthouse built in 1835. This lighthouse was closed in 1954. In winter ice floes whisper as they slither on the tide and current. Imagine them jammed against the stone foundation as they buckle and climb up toward the house. Such was just one of the dangers of living in a lighthouse. Esopus Meadows Lighthouse downstream was knocked off its base by floe ice one winter. (Perhaps even more frightening, imagine a ferry wedged against your lighthouse; that happened, too.)

Downriver stretches the Rhinecliff-Kingston Bridge. Beneath it, down the center of the river from Barrytown to Kingston, runs an underwater ridge for 4½ miles called The Flats. This is one of the primary destinations of the mid-March shad run. The silverbacks swim from the Atlantic Ocean. At that time gill nets are forbidden on the shoals and sandbars of The Flats. The adults return by June to the Atlantic, leaving the young to hatch and mature into one of the largest commercial fisheries in the United States.

Just north of the lighthouse lies another flat, called Green Flats because its wild celery and Eurasian water-milfoil can be seen at low tide. Made up of mud and silt, it stretches north for a mile. Green Flats is an important resting spot for black and mallard ducks. In autumn, you will often see the temporary blinds of duck hunters. Flats like this are also important feeding and resting habitats for fish (including shad and perhaps sturgeon), turtles, and osprey.

The house at the end of the peninsula just to the south is Saugerties Landing, an old steamship stop built on fill to reach the main channel. "Stop" and "landing" are hardly appropriate words, however. The flurry of steamship grandeur in the 1800s and early 1900s crowded the river with large, chugging, band-playing, coal-fired monstrosities of tourist-laden steamships that shouldered aside the wind-sailing sloops and overturned small craft—to the glee of surfing boys—with their rolling wakes. It was a magnificent era, or so they say. On its approach to Saugerties Landing, a steamship would cut its engines, slowing enough to allow the captain to throw his New York City passengers—seeking the peace and pure air of the Catskill mountain houses—with their baggage into a rowboat, sprint for the landing, hand them and their bags off, toss in the return load of passengers with *their* bags, and row hard for the cheering steamer just as it was coasting out of reach about to kick its boilers back into full power.

The preserve is named for the remarkable woman, married to a Turkey Point Coast Guard station attendant, whose concern for the doomed Saugerties Lighthouse resulted in its preservation.

Before you runs the handmade channel of the mouth of Esopus Creek. Born on the flanks of Slide Mountain (see chapter 32, "Giant Ledge"), the Esopus used to join the Hudson estuary nearer the mainland, west of the Coast Guard station you passed earlier. *Esopus* may be an archaic Munsee Lenape word for "creek." An Esopus Indian simply meant a lowlander or river Lenape. When she lived nearby, Ruth Reynolds Glunt described the area: "I have found many arrow and spear heads, as well as odd shaped stones that have been used in hot fires . . . In digging for the foundation we discovered a thick layer of pure white, soft shell . . . we found it was an old Indian shell mound." Archaeological excavations have revealed the area in use by various cultures for 4000 years. This is hardly surprising, considering it is not only on the banks of the Hudson River but also at the confluence of a major tributary, a choice spot still in demand today.

Return to your car the same way you came.

The Shawangunks

Battlement Terrace at Minnewaska State Park. A glacial relict red spruce (Picea rubens) *grows on the left.*

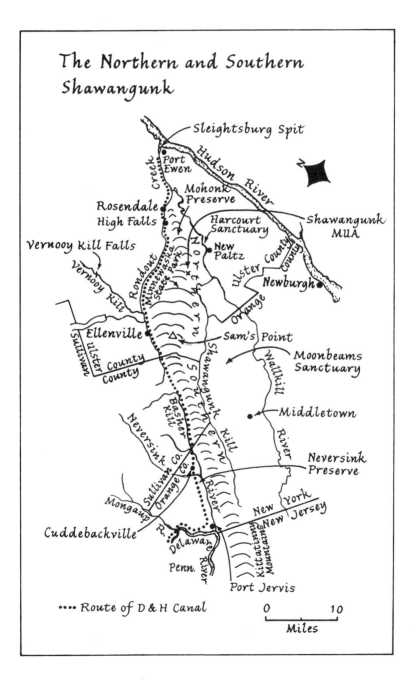

The Northern and Southern Shawangunk

Sleightsburg Spit

Port Ewen

Hudson River

Creek

Mohonk Preserve

Rosendale

High Falls

Harcourt Sanctuary

Shawangunk MUA

Vernooy Kill Falls

Vernooy Kill

Rondout

Minnewaska State Park

New Paltz

Northern

Ulster County

Orange County

Newburgh

Ellenville

Ulster County

Sullivan

County

Sam's Point

Wallkill

Moonbeams Sanctuary

Southern

Shawangunk Kill

Basher Kill

Neversink

Sullivan Co.

Orange Co.

River

Middletown

Neversink Preserve

Wallkill River

Mongaup R.

Cuddebackville

Delaware River

Penn.

New York

New Jersey

Kittatinny Mountains

Port Jervis

···· Route of D & H Canal

0   10

Miles

The Shawangunks

Unlike other mountains in the region that look different when viewed from various directions, the distinctive tilt of the Shawangunk bedrock shows the same ridge profile whether seen from the Hudson Highlands or from the Catskills. Formed 420 million years ago during the Taconic orogeny, or mountain-building episode, which makes it older than the Catskills, the Shawangunk Ridge spans Ulster, Orange, and Sullivan Counties. At its highest the range reaches 2289 feet above sea level at Sam's Point, then gradually diminishes to both the northeast and the southwest in a gently sloping ridge broken by world-class rock-climbing cliff faces.

The Shawangunks are usually spoken of in two sections. The 20-mile-long northern part includes Sam's Point, Minnewaska State Park, Mohonk Preserve, and all the plateau in between, before petering out at the confluence of the Wallkill and Rondout Rivers near Rifton. Five amazingly clear and deep "sky lakes" are located here, including Lake Mohonk and Lake Minnewaska. The 30-mile-long southern section is narrower and lower in overall elevation. It extends past Wurtsboro, where it is commonly called Wurtsboro Ridge; into Pennsylvania, where the ridge becomes high again and is then called the Kittatinny Mountains; and even farther on are the Blue Mountains. The early English called the whole the Blue Mountains (the Catskills were also once called the same). The name in use today, Shawangunk, is a continuation of the original Lenape.

Nicholas Shoumatoff's research among contemporary speakers of the Lenape language indicates "Shawangunk" is derived from words meaning "southern mountains," in the Unami dialect *Shawangee* or *Shawangunkeey*, in the Munsee dialect *Shawangeweng*. It is also possible that the name is derived from *Shiwungeng*, "place of salt." In Lenape, the name is pronounced as it is spelled, in three syllables. The local pronunciation in English is "Shon-gum."

The ridge has lasted for eons because it is capped by pure quartz in a gleaming white conglomerate. The slanting bedrock that makes Minnewaska and Mohonk famous once was termed Shawangunk grit and today is called Shawangunk conglomerate or, simply, quartz (or quartzite) conglomerate. You can see the rounded quartz pebbles cemented within the quartz sandstone. Shallow pockets in this bedrock fill with water and—with extreme slowness—dissolve the sandstone "cement," leaving the pebbles behind within a shallow, blackened bowl. Unlike other forms of bedrock that crumble or flake to help form soil, this dissolving away is the only sort of weathering that occurs on the Shawangunk conglomerate. It lends little if nothing to soil formation or nutrition, and forms such a hard surface that plants can hardly anchor themselves. Shawangunk soil is sparse, shallow, droughty, acidic, and nutrient poor. This, combined with ridge crest weather, talus, and exposed cliff face, makes "the Gunks" a difficult place for colonization by vegetation. Furthermore, the ridge is naturally fire prone. Plants and animals adapted to such conditions have survived and developed a fire-dependent ecosystem like no other in the world, including over 5000 acres of dwarf pitch pine ridge, over 7000 acres of pitch pine–oak heath—where some of the pines are over 300 years of age—and pitch pine–blueberry peat swamp. Rare and endangered species live here, including peregrine falcon, and broom crowberry. There are also black bear, bobcat, and fisher. In addition, bedrock basins and crevices that catch and hold water create a detailed mosaic of varying soil moistures and microclimates. This leads to strange combinations of xeric (extremely dry soil) plants and wetland species beside each other.

New York State and several organizations have flagged the Shawangunk Ridge ecosystem as globally rare and worthy of the highest protection. The Nature Conservancy has designated it as one of the world's 75 "Last Great Places."

Renowned throughout the mountain-climbing world, the white cliffs of the Shawangunk's Trapps and other rock faces provide a multitude of diverse routes for the technical climber. There are beginner, intermediate, and master routes. Devotees leave their homes Friday evening, and those who live in Canada, the Midwest, or the deep South speed through the night for the chance to climb the "Gunks"

Saturday and Sunday before they reload into their cars and drive home by Monday's dawn, barely in time (but happy) for school or work. Mingle with them on the carriageways. Play a game or two of hackeysack. As soon as you leave the climbers, you will have the trails pretty much to yourself.

Only two chapters are included within this section on places for you to visit, yet Minnewaska State Park and Mohonk Preserve are large properties, so there is plenty for you to explore after you visit Lake Awosting and Mill Brook Mountain. Shawangunk Multiple Use Area lies at the foot of the Gunks. Its geology and vegetation make it part of the Wallkill Valley, and so it is included in the lowlands section. Mohonk Mountain House, Smiley Carriageway, and the Ice Caves area are described in chapter 39, "Other Parks."

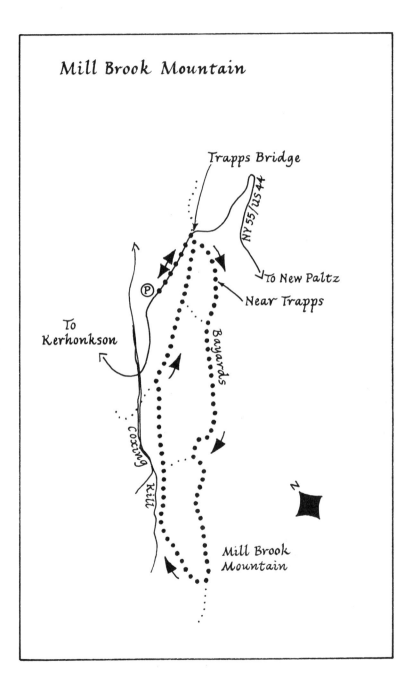

Mill Brook Mountain

Trapps Bridge

NY 55/US 44

To New Paltz

Near Trapps

To Kerhonkson

Bayards

Coxing Kill

Mill Brook Mountain

N

Mill Brook Mountain

Location: New Paltz
Distance: 5¼ miles
Owner: Mohonk Preserve

Come to Mill Brook Mountain in a blueberry year when the bushes droop under loads of round, bursting fruit. The Shawangunks were renowned for their wild blueberries, but that commerce has gone the way of the other Shawangunk industries of barrel hoops, millstones, charcoal, and tanbark.

Wear Vibram soles for the rock and cliff edges of this hike. Sneakers do not allow for the fun of toeing along edges of heights like a fly on the rim of a glass. Visit on a clear day with low humidity for the best views.

This is a full-day hike, but can be shortened by using one of the two red-marked trail cutoffs to form loops.

Access

From New Paltz drive west on NY 299 for 5.8 miles. Turn right onto US 44. Drive 1.5 miles up the escarpment to Trapps Bridge. Many rock climbers, walkers, and cyclists park along the road near Trapps Bridge, but Mohonk Preserve, understanding that this is dangerous practice along a busy highway, asks that you park in its parking lot a third of a mile down the hill on your right. There is a $5-per-person day-use fee. Dogs are allowed but must be under control at all times. For further information on Mohonk Preserve, call 914-255-0919.

Trail

Walk up onto the cinder carriageway of Trapps Bridge and turn south. Go about 50 feet to a left turn on the blue-marked Mill Brook Ridge Trail. This angles up the white rocks following the 22-degree dip of the Shawangunk conglomerate. Gain height with each step to views south and east of the Hudson Highlands, Beacon Range, Schunemunk, Dutchess and Orange Counties, and the lowlands of Ulster. To the west rise the crest of the Shawangunks and some of the Catskill Mountains. Come to this spot in spring or autumn to view the hawk migration.

Pitch pine, chestnut oak and scrub or bear oak, mountain laurel, blueberry, huckleberry, and lichens make up the vegetation. Blueberries and huckleberries are both acid-soil plants of the heath family. The species names are descriptive of their forms: highbush, early low, late low, velvetleaf. "Early" and "late" pertain to when the plants bloom and fruit. However, it can be difficult to distinguish between huckleberry and blueberry and to tell the species apart, especially when they hybridize. The popular method is the taste test, which works, of course, only when there is fruit. Lots of seeds in the fruit means it's a huckleberry, whereas blueberries contain so many tiny seeds you hardly notice them at all. The look-alike deerberry also grows here.

Try to tell species apart. Highbush is the common shoulder-tall blueberry bush with the ridged and twisted limbs whose blue fruit is dusted with white powder. Black highbush has glossy black fruit without the powder and tastes very sweet. Huckleberries, with leaf undersides clad in gold resin, stand no taller than your knee, while some lowbush blueberries reach no taller than your ankle. Whatever they are, they are ready to eat in early July. Different species bloom and ripen over the weeks, extending the eating season into August, a joy that may slow your progress to a halt. "So did you see Mill Brook Mountain?" your friends will ask. "No, we never got past the first mile of blueberry bushes and the second mile of sunny ledges."

The trail follows the ridge crest, affording great views. You are walking on top of the Near Trapps. The presence of red maple and witch-hazel probably indicates pockets of deeper, moist soil trapped within rock crevices. Practice good hiking technique: Step on bare rock, avoiding soil with plants and rock with dense lichens, thus minimizing trampling and erosion damage.

Descend off the Near Trapps into a saddle and keep straight on the blue trail past the red-marked trail. Climb out of the saddle onto the Bayards. Turkey vultures soar along at crest height on mountain thermals. The Shawangunks lie near this scavenger's northern range limit. The sight of them each March heralds spring. Their black silhouette against the white cliffs is often taken as a logo for the Gunks.

The trail weaves back and forth between the woods and the turkey vulture's domain of the rock crest. Far below spreads a field and forest landscape. Conglomerate glacial erratics sit on top of conglomerate bedrock. At the next saddle, just before you come off the Bayards, you can see your destination rising high before you: the imposing pinnacle of Mill Brook Mountain. Climb talus and rock under hemlock back to the high and exposed abode of pitch pine on bedrock barrens. You can see Sky Top in the distance back the way you came. Climb through chestnut oak to a big view east and south and north, west to the opposite Shawangunk ridges. Keep on to higher and higher vantage points. Turkey vultures skim past and just over your head. Ahead grow the white pine trees of Mill Brook Mountain, flagged by the winter's prevailing winds.

The trail leads higher and higher ledge by ledge. Use the trail. The bedrock edge is not continuous and you do not want to trample the fragile flora. Use extreme caution near the edge, especially if you are tired. Continue to the very top, where the red trail comes in at a barrens and the stunted pitch pines grow only in bedrock cracks. Using extreme caution, peer over the edge of tilted conglomerate to the talus fall and treetops far below. Pitch pines and birches grow from cracks in the cliff face. You stand 1200 feet above the valley looking out over "one of the highest sheer cliff-faces east of the Mississippi River," according to Erik Kiviat. The vast panorama shows you nearly all of the Shawangunks, the Catskills, the length of Dutchess County, most of Orange County up to the Hudson Highlands, and most of Ulster County. You can see back over the route you have walked, but you cannot see beyond the first west ridge of Minnewaska State Park.

You will see a carriageway. The blue trail has ended here. Backtrack slightly to the red trail and take it west away from the ledge and into the valley. Do *not* follow the red trail along the crest southward to Gertrude's Nose.

Travel through thick blueberry and huckleberry with a bit of sheep laurel under pitch pines down the steep tilt of the Shawangunk face. Shortly, come to the beginning of the blue trail and turn right onto it. Chestnut oak increases in frequency and pitch pine decreases until finally it disappears and you are in a mixed deciduous forest of oaks, black birch, moosewood, hemlock, red maple, and mountain laurel. Listen for the faint trickling sound of the Coxing Kill off into the woods to your left. Bushwhack over to enjoy the water—cold on even the most sweltering summer day. Mossy rocks ring green-gold pools of clear water. Round white and pink quartz pebbles line the bottom, freed from their dissolved conglomerate matrix. Rest and dabble your feet. Turn over underwater rocks to look for hellgrammites. Be sure to put the rocks back the way you found them.

The trail leads into lush, moist, green woods. Pass the red trail, keeping on the blue. At the carriageway, turn right for the return to Trapps Bridge.

Lake Awosting

Location: Minnewaska State Park
Distance: 10 miles
Owner: State of New York

Y ou can hike, picnic, cross-country ski, and swim at 10,600-acre Minnewaska State Park. Minnewaska has become popular among mountain bikers, who enjoy some of the finest carriageways in the region past spectacular and dangerous clifftop views.

There are miles of trails to explore at this state park. Many people tramp the 3 hot and dusty miles in to the unique swimming beach at wild Awosting Lake, perhaps the park's second most popular destination after turquoise, sparkling Lake Minnewaska itself. This chapter describes a combination of carriageway and footpath walking past scented leaves and flowers to Awosting Lake, visiting Rainbow Falls and glacial relict spruces along the way.

Access

From the Wallkill River bridge as you leave New Paltz on NY 299, travel 5.9 miles to a right onto US 44/NY 55 West. Follow 4.9 miles past the main state park entrance ($4 per car) to another entrance on your left, the large, dirt Awosting parking lot. There is a per-person charge during the winter, but in all other seasons parking here is free. Locked gates open at 9 AM daily, with closing times posted seasonally (generally around 8:30 or 9 PM in summer, 5 PM in winter). Dogs are permitted if on a leash except in winter, when they are not allowed in the park at all. For more information, call 914-255-0752.

Trail

At the far end of the parking lot, follow the dirt Awosting Carriageway, marked with black diamonds. Just as you begin your walk, pass a slope of dry bedrock and a spare growth of pitch pines on your left,

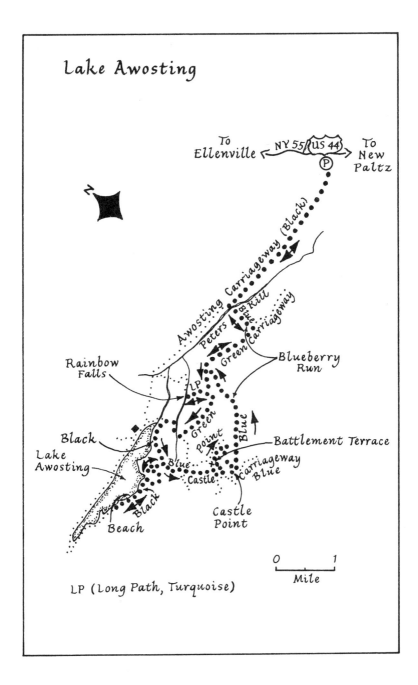

Lake Awosting

a taste of barrens to come. Walk a dry corridor of sunlight thick with aromatic, sun-loving herbs.

Under summer sunbeams, pungent oils evaporate from the herbal leaves to float over the trail. The fragrance of sweet fern bruised by the passing of cyclists fills the air. You only need to run your open palm across the bushtops to scent your hands. Dry waves of aromatic heat lift up from hay-scented ferns, highbush blueberry, hardhack *(Spiraea tomentosa)*, witch-hazel, pearly everlasting *(Anaphalis margaritacea)*, and white snakeroot *(Eupatorium rugosum)*.

In a couple of miles, watch on your left for the narrow footpath marked in blue that is Blueberry Run. Watch with care; it is easy to miss this turnoff. Follow Blueberry Run down to the gold-shot water of the Peters Kill that tumbles across the sloping Shawangunk conglomerate bedrock. On the banks grows the tall rosebay *(Rhododendron maximum)*, our native great rhododendron. Cross the bridge and follow up the slanted bedrock. At the carriageway, marked with a green diamond, turn right. At the power line, inspect the barren bedrock on your left where it rises from the roadway for the shiny slickness of glacial polish. The level carriageway (be alert for swift bicyclists) runs along the ridge at a height. Keep straight on this green-marked road even as the blue footpath turns left.

Find the right turnoff for Rainbow Falls. The turquoise-marked trail (actually part of the Long Path) descends steeply beneath overhanging beech limbs. Cross a small brook and head downhill through hemlocks with practically no undergrowth. You hear the falls echoing ahead and smell the water on the cooling air; the microclimate has changed. Cross another brook and climb a short but steep talus fall to pretty Rainbow Falls, small but enchanting. Three streams of water dribble over a ledge slapping the stones at your feet.

Return the way you came to the carriageway and turn right to continue. The turquoise Long Path turns left, but you keep straight on the carriageway. At the junction with the black-marked carriageway coming in on your right, keep straight on what is now the continuation of the black carriageway. Ahead, see the openness through the trees that signals the lake. Bedrock and pitch pine appear, and you come to the ledge and the magnificent view: across the lake to the

Looking south down the length of Lake Awosting's swirling turquoise waters toward Sam's Point. When the sun is not dazzling you, you can see that the low-browed Shawangunk ridges are studded with windswept white pines.

long stretch of the Shawangunk ridge lifting south toward its highest elevation at Sam's Point. Some of the Catskills loom on the horizon to your right.

In mid-August, you will smell *Clethra* on the wind. Sweet pepperbush, as it is also known, rings the lake. Even more grows on the surrounding hills in watered soil pockets. If you investigate the bedrock outcrops carefully, you might find mountain sandwort (*Minuartia groenlandica*). This tundra plant exists in the Shawangunks as a glacial relict, a plant that grew on the plateau—probably in abundance—in the chilly wake of the glacial recession and grows here still in colder spots where conditions remain similar to that postglacial time.

Follow the black Awosting Carriageway, a right turn downhill toward Awosting Beach through pitch pine, then hemlock, to a shore of *Clethra* humming with bees, beetles, and butterflies. Follow the road to the unique beach of slanting bedrock. Here the rock looks white, but under the exceptionally clear water turns red and green.

Swimming is allowed here only when a lifeguard is on duty. Along the road and the beach you can find northern bog species: leatherleaf *(Chamaedaphne calyculata),* tallbush blueberry, sheep laurel, sweet gale (the aromatic *Myrica gale),* marsh St. Johnswort *(Hypericum virginicum),* and swamp azalea (whose sticky white flowers in late spring smell intoxicatingly sweet).

Return back uphill and turn right on the blue-diamond Castle Point Carriageway. Pass pockets of wetlands and dark pools of water within tubs of bedrock. The incongruous juxtaposition of wet and dry species is especially apparent when Castle Point comes into view ahead. On your right is a xeric pitch pine barrens. On your left is a wet area populated by both dry and wet soil species dominated by mountain-holly *(Nemopanthus mucronata).* At the four-way intersection, bear left toward Castle Point on the blue-diamond carriageway. This loops beneath the white cliffs. When you see more cliffs on your left, look at the darkest conifers in the wet hollow. These are red spruce, another glacial relict. Distinguish spruce from hemlock by its rigid point of a top. The leader on hemlock drapes to the side. Mountain-ash further designates this as a cooler microclimate.

The carriageway switchbacks up to the ledges. From Battlement Terrace and then Castle Point, gain tremendous and sweeping panoramas of Orange and Ulster Counties and beyond. Leave the carriageway at the blue-marked trail, which begins just before Castle Point and leads away from the ledge. Backtrack and find this trail, called Blueberry Run, infrequently marked in the beginning. Follow the white glacier-slickened bedrock and the cairns, small piles of stones that mark the trail, through pitch pines, heath, and bracken fern. This is another of those intimate footpaths that involve the hiker with the landscape. The trail bed has worn through the meager layer of soil to expose the white bedrock beneath.

As soon as Blueberry Run leaves the ledges, it meets with deeper soil that grows a forest. The trail leads through a succession of vegetation types caused by changes in the proximity of bedrock to the soil surface. At the green carriageway, turn right. Past the power line, turn left to retrace your steps on Blueberry Run, turning right onto Awosting Carriageway for the return to your car.

The Catskills

Morning dewdrops

The Catskills

They were once called the Blue Mountains, supposedly because of their dark fur of vast hemlock forest. Their current name, "Catskills," comes from the Dutch for "tomcat creek," according to some. Other stories say it was the surname of a Dutch landowner, or a corrupted Native Lenape word. No one really knows. And they are not real mountains at all, in the sense of having been pushed up. The Catskills are actually a plateau of uplifted, consolidated sediments eroded into mountain shapes by streams. You can find fossils, ripple marks of sandbars, rounded beach stones, and trim layers of streambed deposits in the various Catskill limestones, shales, conglomerates, and sandstones.

Historic Native folks knew the Catskills well, some say mainly as a hunting and gathering territory. Even today, the Catskills are perhaps best known to Native technologists as the historic home of Catskill and Coxsackie chert, a fine, workable flint. When Europeans arrived in the Hudson Valley, they kept away from the forbidding, cold, and rocky peaks. Queen Anne of England did grant a patent for much of the hills in 1708 to Johannis Hardenburgh and six others, but for over a century Europeans settled the more gentle and fertile lowlands to north, south, east, and west. Then they noticed the hemlocks.

The tannin in hemlock bark tans an animal hide into leather. Tanneries sprang up along Catsill Mountain creeks, importing hides and polluting the clear waters. By the late 1880s all but the most inaccessible of the Catskill hemlocks were gone and the tanneries were forced to close. Since only the bark from butt to first limb was removed by the bark peelers, the Blue Mountains became gray and brown with standing hemlock skeletons and rotting logs, then flashed with the red of wildfires, followed by a bright green of new hardwood growth. Today, the Catskill forests are oak dominant in the lowest elevations; an association of sugar maple, beech, and yellow birch on the middle, moist slopes; yellow birch and black cherry on the upper slopes; and balsam fir, red spruce, and mountain-ash on the highest peaks. On the crests the trees are stunted, a function of shallow soil depth, exposure to storm winds, and a low mean annual temperature. The harsh, cool climate fosters the growth of more northerly species of plants. Biogeochemically, the summits of the high peaks are islands of northern climate and soil conditions that foster the continued growth of boreal woods. Only in the deep folds of mountain ravines remain the dark-cloaked hemlocks.

With the forest gone, farmers cleared remaining stumps, and lumbering felled what timber remained or regrew. Charcoal burning and hoop shaving for cooperage used the second- and third-growth woods. Bluestone quarrying (often by deluded prospectors searching for gold) and small precious metal mines were dug here and there. Water-powered mills were established on creeks for grist, sawing timber, carding, and tanning. The small, family hill farms scraped along. Immigrants newly arrived in New York City signed on as Catskill farm tenants. They burned the woods all winter, sold the potash or white salts for soapmaking in summer, pastured dairy cows, gathered and sold wild medicinals such as wintergreen and ginseng, and cut a bit of timber to survive. Slopes denuded by tanning and farming brought severe floods every spring, washing away the hill soil.

The consumptive population of New York City discovered the "clean" air and waters of the Catskills, and the grand-hotel era flourished in the late 1800s and early 1900s. Changes in the dairy industry after World War I eliminated most of the hill farms, which fell into ruins or burned. Industry waned and much of that population drifted away. As the hills revegetated, the floods subsided and appreciation for the hills' aesthetic value grew.

The 705,000 acres of the Catskills are wilder today than they have been in 200 years, yet they are not wilderness. Past use still marks the landscape. Farm ruins, quarries, and lumber roads slowly disappear beneath the healing regrowth of the forest. The mountains today are a mosaic of private lands and state property, the latter legislated to be left "forever wild" with "no works of man." Many of the walks that follow lie within designated "wilderness areas," which

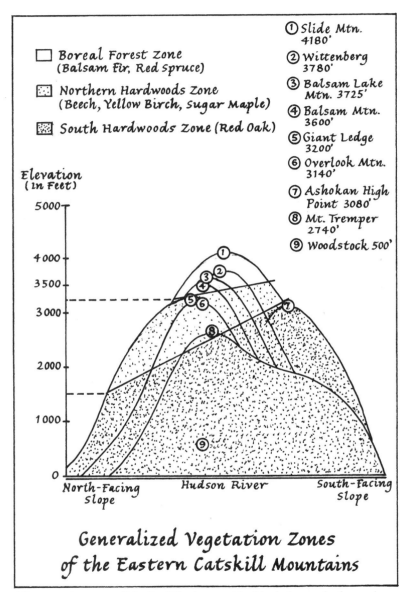

Generalized Vegetation Zones of the Eastern Catskill Mountains

The vegetation zones of the Catskills change with altitude just as the forests change when you travel north. Every 1000 feet of elevation gain corresponds roughly to 200 miles of latitude change northward. The higher Catskills can support three forest zones: southern hardwoods, northern hardwoods, and boreal woods. The highest summits represent islands of Canadian shield climate and soil conditions. There are local exceptions to the occurrence of these zones.

are maintained with a minimal intrusion of human activity. Such large landholdings provide an enormous and largely undisturbed reservoir of wildlife habitat. Once there were moose and wolves, yet today there are still resident populations of black bear, porcupine, ermine, mink, otter, snowshoe hare, bobcat, wild turkey, beaver, fisher, coyote, deer, ruffed grouse, and many other animals. Neotropical birds that likewise require large tracts of land, such as scarlet tanager, rose-breasted grosbeak, red-eyed vireo, Louisiana waterthrush, black-and-white warbler, and black-throated blue warbler, breed and nest successfully.

Nowadays, tourism and recreation are the main industries of the Catskills. The nearly 280,000 acre Catskill Forest Preserve, delineated by an imaginary "blue line" on the official map, is visited mostly on weekends and holidays. The voluntary register boxes in 1993 recorded 34,000 visitors to just the Ulster County portion of the preserve. It is estimated that this figure must be doubled to represent an actual-use number. Most of these visitors went to the Slide Mountain area, the Catskills' highest peak.

You may camp anywhere in the Catskills so long as you are below 3500 feet in elevation from December 22 to March 20; always at least 150 feet from a trail, road, or water; and careful never to start a campfire. You may also stay in numerous lean-to shelters with campfire rings and state-run, public campgrounds. Practice ethical woodsman camping. Never damage even a fern by your temporary visit.

Carry good trail maps. The New York–New Jersey Trail Conference publishes the best. Dress properly. Beware of the weather. Summer thunder rolls echoing around the hills like a giant ball bounced from slope to slope, accompanied by fierce winds and hail. Spring and fall snow squalls turn the warm high peaks into winter. Compared to "real" mountains, like the Rockies or the Alps, the Catskills may seem small and tame. I am certain that thousands of visitors have calmly walked up Slide Mountain and back down again without mishap. Yet in my experience, as often as not real mountain calamities follow the trails up Slide and other hills. The Catskills are not a place to take lightly. Slide Mountain is not just another hill.

For example: My first climb up Slide was with my undergraduate terrestrial ecology class come to see the red spruce on the Wittenberg, and Slide's balsam fir stands. Strong and eager environmental science students climbed Slide from the Wittenberg—the more difficult side—when one young woman slid on the steep bedrock and hit her head so hard we wondered if she was going to go into convulsions. She spent the day dazed.

John Burroughs wrote of his climbs as "a sort of laying siege to Slide." Of course he insisted on a bushwhack up the rockslide itself, whereas today we have the convenience of a jeep path on a gentler slope. But, still, folk often struggle on the ascent. I had a friend who tried five times to climb Slide as part of a 2-night, 3-day loop over Giant Ledge, Slide, Cornell, and the Wittenberg. Five tries, success only twice. Three times sudden snow and frigid winds forced him to turn back. Burroughs likewise commented on this: "Round pellets of snow began to fall, and we came off the mountain on the 10th of June in a November storm and temperature." I have watched my friend shake his fist at the mountain as men do in Yukon mountain movies—the lone man below the inaccessible prize of the precipice—"I'll be back!" When he finally did succeed, his dog attacked a porcupine, one of many on the crest, and got a pawful of quills. It had to be hand-carried off the mountain, and it was not a small dog.

My most recent visit to Slide Mountain was on a sunny October day. All the autumn hills spread golden. Snow squalls suddenly swept over the headlands and, once on the summit, the temperature dropped, the pleasant sky socked in with cold clouds, blanking the view, and it began to snow heavily. As I came off the mountain back into autumn and sunny skies, I questioned people along the trail: Had they seen the snow, the first of the year? No one had any idea what I was even talking about. In the valley and on the slopes, the warm autumn sun had been shining all along.

Vernooy Kill Falls

Location: Kerhonkson
Distance: 3.6 miles
Owner: State of New York

This popular summer swimming hole can be reached from either Kerhonkson in the Rondout Valley or Dymond Road in the Peekamoose Valley. This description leads from Kerhonkson. Bring your swimsuit.

Access

From US 209 in Kerhonkson, turn north onto Ulster County 3/Samsonville Road at a state education sign concerning a colonial fort. Go for 3.5 miles. At the sign for Veritas Villa, bear left onto Lower Cherrytown Road across a stream. Go for 1.4 miles. At the intersection with Cherrytown Road and Upper Cherrytown Road, bear right onto Upper Cherrytown. Go 3.1 miles to marked parking on the right. You will know you are approaching when you see the turquoise "mailbox" that flags the Long Path. Snowmobiles use this path in winter.

Trail

After the dry drive through the overbright Shawangunk in the car, you stand at the trailhead on an old woods road becalmed with verdant silence and shadowed hemlocks dripping damp. You are just over the Blue Line, on the very edge of the Catskills, and they are unmistakable—wild, backed by thousands of acres of forest; there is an anchoring and undisturbed weight, a presence, to these woods.

The trail is marked with orange snowmobile and blue hiking disks, even though this is part of the Long Path. Begin in moist mixed woods of white pine; hemlock; chestnut, red, and black oak; red, sugar, and striped maple; yellow birch; witch-hazel; and mountain laurel. What a mix! As you walk you can also find cottonwood, tulip-

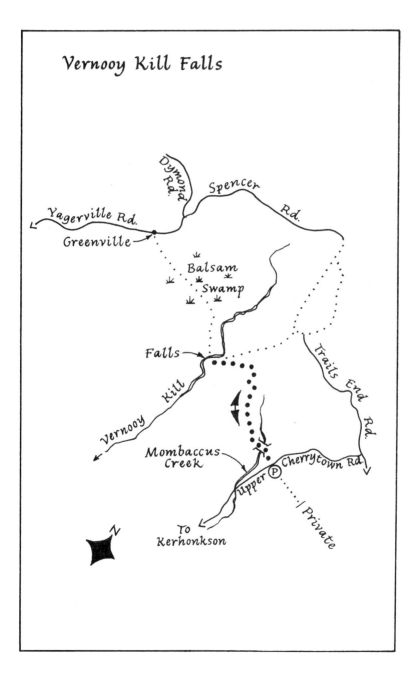

Vernooy Kill Falls

tree, beech, paper birch, and stems of doomed American chestnut suckering from old roots. Hemlock form whole groves with nothing beneath them but the dead-needled floor.

Cross Mombaccus Creek and follow it upstream a short way before leaving it to climb a moderate slope. Climb out of the abode of hemlock into mixed deciduous woods with a high amount of cottonwood. You are traversing the slope that separates Mombaccus Creek from the Vernooy Kill. It is not an overlong climb, yet enough to whet the appetite for a cool waterfall. Brush the edge of a hemlock stand that reaches up a section of cool slope, then pass into a predominantly beech and black-and-yellow birch woods combined with red oak. The forest composition keeps changing, because the soil moisture and exposure change as you round the ridge.

After a late summer's rain you will find many mushrooms. The red *Russula* with the white gills and stem is one of the edibles. *Amanita muscaria,* fly mushroom, with yellow or orange hood speckled with white warts, is the toadstool often depicted in fairy tale book illustrations. It was imbibed by festival-mad Siberian tribespeople in the past and is the supposed source of the ancient *berserker* rage, deadly to most folk. Far more lethal is the shining destroying angel, so singly perfect a mushroom. A child who has eaten just a fragment of the cap of *Amanita virosa* will die. At first nothing seems to have happened—a pure white innocent mushroom. Half a day passes with no ill effect. By the time the vomiting and fits begin, the liver has already been destroyed.

Mountain laurel crowds the red maple, paper birch, and red oak woods. You can hear the falls up ahead. Yet again the forest composition changes, to white pine, black cherry, yellow birch, and red maple with lowbush blueberry, grasses, and ferns. Sign in at the trail register.

Even in times of severe drought, cold Vernooy Kill runs, dropping about 60 feet over Catskill shale ledges in a series of cascades. Actually, these are the upper falls of the Vernooy Kill—named for the Vernooey family. Cornelius Vernooey left Holland with his wife and child in 1664. They were among the first European settlers in the area. The Vernooey family operated a gristmill below the falls from

The amber upper pool is at its deepest right beneath the waterfall.

the early 1700s until 1809. You can still see a 15- to 20-foot-high stone wall that was part of the mill. Be careful while you explore southward; there are two rattlesnake dens in the area.

Each successive, gold-shot pool upstream spreads wider and deeper. I cannot touch bottom in the upper pool. The golden tea color comes from tannin leached from the roots and fallen needles of hemlocks. White bubbles are whipped saponins released from decayed leaves. This is a beautiful, mossy stream to dabble in. I am entranced by the fall and swish of current. The woods, likewise, are lovely.

If you still feel like walking, you can cross the bridge and follow the Greenville Trail to Balsam Swamp, the balsam bog headwaters of Vernooy Kill. This red spruce–balsam fir swamp is a relict of the glacial age and contains other boreal species, including creeping snowberry *(Gaultheria hispidula),* sheep laurel, mountain-holly, and wild raisin *(Viburnum cassinoides).* The Long Path continues upstream on the side you came in on for 8 steep miles to Bull Run on Peekamoose Road. The return to your car is back the way you came.

Ashokan High Point

Location: Olive
Distance: 7.5 miles
Owner: State of New York

This is a blueberry walk, a deep hollow walk, a panorama hike. Enjoy all of these on the Kanape Trail to Ashokan High Point (3080 feet above sea level). Come on a clear morning and plan to spend the day lazing in the high blueberry meadows—just reward after a long climb. This is a popular place on weekends.

Access

From West Shokan drive 4.2 miles along Ulster County 42/Peekamoose Road to parking on your right marked for Kanape Brook.

Trail

Cross the road and backtrack slightly to a right turn past a barrier into the woods on an unmarked trail. (There are plans to mark this trailhead with signs.) Cross Kanape Brook on a wooden footbridge and you are on an old town road first built in 1835. This was once the only way through the mountains from Watson Hollow of today's Peekamoose Road to the Rondout Valley. It was called Freeman Avery Road, named for Orson Avery, who, along with John Jones Canape, was the first farmer in the area. In the 1930s the road was rebuilt by the Civilian Conservation Corps (CCC) as a fire truck trail, used until the 1960s by men hired to combat fires set by berry pickers on top of Hoopole Mountain, a knob northwest of Ashokan High Point.

Parallel the tumbling Catskill stream known for its pure water quality. If you watch with care you will notice signs of hardscrabble farms: stone walls, cellar holes, rock heaps, foundations, old road cuts,

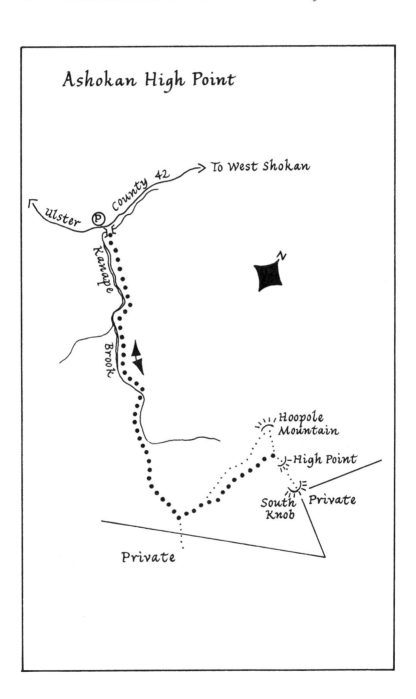

Ashokan High Point

and the remains of a dam. Foundations of bark-peeler huts on the left slope are even older.

The ravine deepens. Kanape Brook rushes beneath dark hemlocks while you walk an easy uphill stroll through deciduous woods. Pass a healthy Norway spruce plantation planted by the CCC in an attempt to reforest farmland newly purchased by the state. The uphill stretches become moderately steep. Keep on the main track. Where the trail crosses Kanape Brook near a designated camping site, a hemlock and a Norway spruce grow on opposite banks side by side. Here you see how they look when both grow in optimal conditions. In the shadowed woods they can be confounded by the beginner, but here it is simple to see their differences.

Enter a Norway spruce plantation with absolutely no undergrowth, followed by an extensive hemlock stand. Imagine how the Catskills looked before the bark peelers destroyed the vast hemlock forests. Kanape Brook lies within the Sundown Wild Forest. "Sundown" is the old name for the area and comes from the perpetual gloom beneath the tall hemlocks that once populated the region.

Climb a moderate slope to a level col where you encounter crest-type vegetation among the shortened red oaks and red maples: lowbush blueberry, huckleberry, mountain laurel, American chestnut (suckers on old roots), and white pine seedlings and saplings. Watch for the fork where you leave the old road to bear left and begin your climb. Do not continue on the old road since it leads onto private property closed to hikers. Soon chestnut oak and bracken fern appear. Pass an old bulldozer road that forks left. This leads to Hoopole Mountain. The climb steepens and towhees call off in the laurel. The oaks get shorter. The climb pitches steeply upward. Six times level terraces fool you into thinking you have reached the summit, only to reveal yet another steep climb.

The summit view off the ledge where once stood a triangulation tower for surveying shows the Shawangunk ridge south to the Beacons, Schunemunk, and the Hudson Highlands. The year 1888 seemed to be especially popular for carving graffiti into the ledge.

Two unique knobs flank Ashokan High Point's summit. The one to the northwest is called Hoopole Mountain. The other—which some people call Little High Point, and others Blueberry Hill—lies to the southeast and is on the edge of state property. Both have superior views and are covered with a dense growth of the fattest, sweetest blueberries you have ever tasted. Blueberries and most heaths are crest, fire-adapted plants able to withstand light brushfires on mountaintops that tend to kill other shrubs and trees. Annual burning is the accepted method to encourage blueberry takeover. This halts the successional process and maintains vegetation at the heath stage.

Berry pickers burned both knobs of High Point from the 1890s until the 1970s to gain a marketable harvest. In fact, they found two ways to make a living. The area ranger tells the story he learned from a Mr. Shultis, who grew up in the area. Berry pickers hiked up on top of one of High Point's knobs and arranged a lighted candle protected by a rock from drafts and couched in a circle of dry leaves. Then they hiked off the mountain and waited at the local gin mill downstream. When the call went out for firefighters, the question was always asked: Who could possibly have started yet another fire when everyone knew no one had been up on the mountain for hours? The state paid firefighters in those days. Nowadays the incentive to start fires is eliminated. The state employs only volunteers.

To reach the northwest knob of Hoopole Mountain (named for the cooperage industry that shaved hoops here), take the side trail directly opposite the summit view so that you are headed northwest through the stunted red oak woods (watch on your left for the pool of a black bear wallow) and just keep going. First you pass a view to the west of nearby Mombaccus and Little Rocky Mountains. Continue and you arrive at blueberry heaven. Blueberry's continued prevalence shows the long-term effect of systematic burning on a harsh, mountaintop environment. Of course, the effect does not last forever if it is not maintained. Eventually these meadows will grow up into red oak woods. In these meadows you gain fabulous views north and northwest of, from left to right: Peekamoose, Table, Lone, Rocky, Balsam Cap and Friday with Slide Mountain rising behind, Cornell, Wittenberg, and Terrace Mountains.

To reach the south knob, from the summit view go straight over the ledge southeast toward the Shawangunk and keep going steeply

The plantation of Norway spruce (Picea abies) *along Kanape Brook early in the morning*

downhill over ledges. So many folks have done this that there are herd paths that you can follow. Reach the narrow pass of Wagon Wheel Gap or Notch and head up again to emerge on top of the knob. The views from here are superior and spacious. Mombaccus Mountain, on your immediate left, slopes down to the Rondout Valley. Across the horizon stretches the entire Shawangunk, with Sky Top at Mohonk Mountain House dead center. To your left spread Ashokan

Reservoir, the Hudson Highlands, the Beacons, and the south Taconics. To the north is the Devil's Path, those distinctive shapes of the northeastern Catskills. Ashokan High Point's bulk blocks the view west. Hawks, turkey vultures, and falcons ride the thermals up from the valley floor and sail over the knob. Yellow paint on the rocks denotes the state boundary. Please do not trespass on private property. Beware thunderheads blowing over the Catskills and colliding with the Hudson Valley trough of summer haze. This makes for terrific thunderstorms of lightning, wind, and hail atop High Point.

In addition to the blueberries, there are also huckleberries, red oaks so stunted they might be mistaken for scrub oak, mountain laurel, a substantial amount of bearberry, or kinnikinnick, growing among its heath kin, and a bit of three-leaved cinquefoil rooted in crevices.

If you visit each knob you will gain the 360-degree view that High Point affords. On the return, back the way you came, with the sun high in the afternoon, the hemlock ravine of Kanape Brook is gorgeous.

Overlook Mountain

Location: Woodstock
Distance: 4 miles
Owner: State of New York

A popular lookout and walk among locals, Overlook Mountain's fire tower is no longer open to the public. The first story of stairs has been removed. However, a nearby, lesser-known rock ledge affords a tremendous view, and you can explore the ruins of a large hotel near the summit.

Access

From the village center of Woodstock, take Ulster County 33 north toward the Glasco Turnpike. At the stop sign keep straight through on Meads Mountain Road. Climb steeply to the mountaintop. Parking is on your right.

Trail

Before you begin your walk, visit the Tibetan Buddhist monastery and the Catholic chapel. You may be too tired to appreciate these unique sites after your walk. From the parking lot, cross Meads Mountain Road and walk beneath the red and gold Tibetan arch. Follow signs for the office and gain permission to enter the temple (shorts and skimpy shirts not allowed: It is worthwhile to throw on a pair of pants or a skirt for the visit, then leave them behind in your car when you start your hike). Karma Triyana Dharmachakra is the North American seat of a main branch of Tibetan Buddhism. This authentic, cathedral-like temple looks exactly as they do in Asia.

Next, walk down Meads Mountain Road back the way you motored for a short distance, just past the Tibetan monastery to a small wooden chapel in the woods on your right. It is always open, an unusual Orthodox Catholicism of an ancient order. If stepping into the Tibetan temple feels like entering another world, walking into the

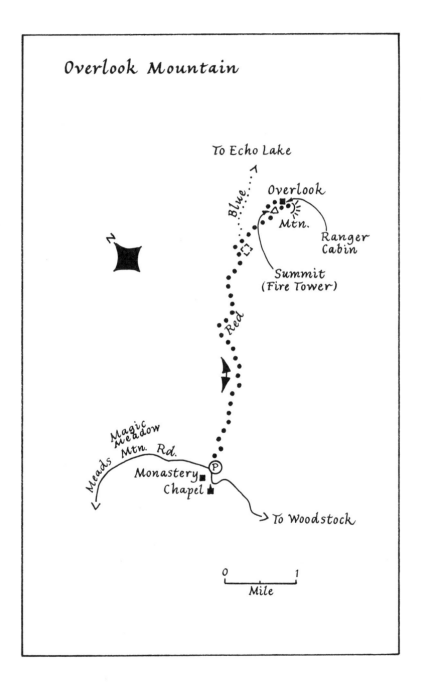

shadowed, wood-carved chapel feels like entering another time: Europe's medieval ages.

Then on to Overlook Mountain. Walk up the red-marked dirt road and sign in at the trail register. The hike climbs uphill all the way. Near the summit you come upon the ruins. Destroyed by fire in 1924, Overlook Mountain House was built in 1878 upon the ruins of its 1871 predecessor, also destroyed by fire. The concrete walls you see were poured in 1928, but the project was abandoned midstream and never completed. Slim, bright paper birches and fluttering cottonwoods grow in the soil on the hotel floor. Keep on the road past the ruins and the communications tower. Just beyond and opposite the cement pool of water grows a lovely ash grove with an herb cover of goldenrod. Sixty-nine species of goldenrod grow in the Northeast. How many different species can you find here?

Immediately beyond this you arrive at the junction with the blue-marked trail, which leads to Echo Lake. Keep straight on the red trail for 0.5 mile to the summit. As you walk, you will see ledges off to your right. The trees on that side are all short and gnarled, indicative of harsh living conditions. The stunted forest is made up of a mixture of red oak, paper and yellow birch, beech, red maple, and the red-berried mountain-ash (also called rowan, *Sorbus americana,* formerly *Pyrus).* This odd combination may seem inexplicable unless you venture down the blue trail toward Echo Lake. The northern hardwood forest on this cooler, moist, north-facing slope contains beech, yellow birch, sugar maple, ash, moosewood, hobblebush *(Viburnum lantanoides,* formerly *alnifolium),* wild sarsaparilla, and oxalis. The south-facing slope, which is warmer and dryer, supports a southern hardwood, red oak forest. The two mix across the Overlook summit. Pass a quarry on your left being colonized by grasses and herbs.

A ranger cabin and the closed fire tower at the top stand among the trees. Here you can find lowbush blueberry, hobblebush, and a few balsam fir in token of the 3140-foot elevation, scant yards below the altitude that fosters Catskill boreal forest. Three vegetation zones normally separated by sheer altitude are thus represented on Overlook due to differences in slope microclimate. In summer there is a partial view, which improves when the leaves fall. It is too bad the tower is closed—the view must be grand (people manage to monkey up the spare metal beams anyway). But no matter; there is another way.

Behind the ranger cabin, follow the footpath that leads to the cliff with a vast view of the Hudson River winding southward. Starting from your left, see Saugerties and beyond that the Hudson River, Dutchess and Columbia Counties with the south Taconics on the horizon at the Massachusetts/Connecticut/New York border. On very clear days you can even see the Berkshires and the Housatonic Highlands. Following to your right find Kingston and its bridge. The Hudson River curves into Crum Elbow and then disappears behind Shaupeneak and the Marlboro Hills. On the south horizon loom the Beacon Range and the Hudson Highlands, stretching westward until your eye arrives in the foreground of the view looking over all the northern Shawangunks, including Sky Top, Eagle Cliff, and the vast, high Minnewaska/High Point plateau. In the foreground of that stretches Ashokan Reservoir and then, farther right, some of the Catskills of Ulster County. If you hike up here on a muggy day, you will be lucky to find Ashokan Reservoir.

The cliff bedrock is littered with graffiti. Most have been scratched on with crude tools, but the finest date from the Victorian, grand mountain-hotel years when every hiker, it seems, carried a chisel and hammer with which to carve tidy names and dates.

Search the bedrock cracks for three-toothed cinquefoil. This tundra plant roots in the soil trapped within fractures. If you dare to peer over the cliff edge, you will find the rock encrusted with rock tripe lichen. Watch for birds of prey. They hunt along the air currents along this escarpment. The long wings of large turkey vultures are held in a distinctive V shape that tilts and shakes from side to side as they soar without a wing flap. Buteos, one family of hawks, have heavy bodies and short, wide tails. A flash of rusty tail as a buteo circles marks a red-tailed hawk. Accipiters, another type of hawk, have thinner bodies and long, narrow tails and short wings. They tend to streak by in a straight line of flight. Falcons look like jet planes, streamlined with long, pointed wings and tails.

You can follow the narrow path along the ledges back to the hotel ruins. This is the highest elevation at which a small and rare

A hidden path leads to this ledge with a view over the old Plain of Shokan, where Esopus Creek was dammed to create the Ashokan Reservoir (seen in the background).

butterfly, the falcate orangetip, has been observed fluttering. In May, the females lay tiny orange eggs on the flowers and seedpods of lyre-leaved rock cress *(Arabis lyrata)* plants growing in the ledges. Retrace your steps down the mountain along the road.

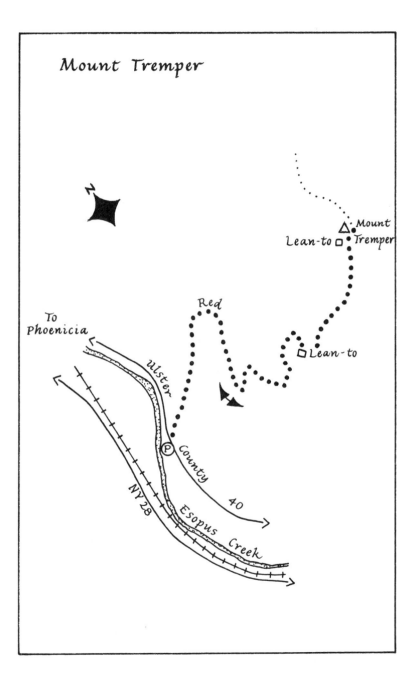

Mount Tremper

Mount Tremper

Lean-to

Red

To Phoenicia

Ulster

Lean-to

P

County

40

NY 28

Esopus Creek

Mount Tremper

Location: Phoenicia
Distance: 5.5 miles
Owner: State of New York

Compared to other, wilder Catskill mountains, Mount Tremper seems tamed. The scars of past use persist. Its flanks are roped by abandoned roads and scarred by bluestone quarries. It is settled by two lean-tos and surmounted by a fire tower. The main reason to climb it—the 360-degree view from the tower—is no longer applicable since the first set of stairs was removed and the rest of the ailing structure is unsafe. The visitor can gain partial views through the trees when the leaves are down, but that's about it.

So why come here? To walk in the woods, camp at the lean-tos, and explore the bluestone quarry. Besides, do you really need a reason to climb a mountain? Mount Tremper is steep, but the well-built road, part of the Long Path, switchbacks and uses moderate slopes to gain height with ease.

Access

From Phoenicia, drive 1.6 miles southeast on Ulster County 40 to a parking pull-off on the streamside marked "Esopus Creek Public Fishing Stream."

Trail

Fish-full Esopus Creek runs over rounded cobbles past the hip-waders of fly-anglers. The trailhead is across the street. In summer Mount Tremper is a dry trip, despite two springs, so get your fill of the sight of water now. Sign in at the register box just within the woods line, which announces you have entered the Phoenicia–Mt. Tobias Wild Forest. The old woods road, marked in red, was used at different times as a carriage track, a timber path, a quarry road, and a jeep path for servicing the fire tower. It climbs gradually through

*Water-drop trickles down the face of the main cut
at the bluestone quarry at Mount Tremper*

the northern hardwood community of hemlock, yellow birch, sugar maple, beech, witch-hazel, and striped maple, with a few large ash, some basswood and hop hornbeam, and, now and then, a white pine.

About a mile from the trailhead you will see a mound of rocks in a sunny opening on your left. Keep on the woods road until it brings you on a level with the bluestone quarry. Find the washed-out old access road, now an obscure footpath, that leads to more stone piles. Hikers have played here, building walls, shelters, tables, benches, and a large fireplace. In fact, this quarry must look like what the abandoned quarry in Saugerties looked like before Harvey Fite began building his environmental sculpture garden, Opus 40. (For information on Opus 40, phone 914-246-3400.) Explore back to the main cut, a sheer wall of smooth bluestone cliff. To either side in the woods there are older, smaller cuts. As you wander around, just be careful always to look before you place a hand or a foot among the rocks. Rattlesnakes have been found here.

Quarrying businesses began mining bluestone in the Catskills in 1832. In the wintertime the frozen soil was blasted away to expose the top of the ledge. Cleaving of the beds went on in the warmer months. The natural breakage of these ledges runs at right angles, allowing the stone to be lifted intact in sheets *if* not too brittle. That was the catch, the "miner's gamble." The answer could not be known until the wedges were driven. Quarries like this one were small businesses usually worked by two to five men who leased the site from the landowner. The hard work barely paid off after the cost of transportation to the stone mill, sometimes half the value of the load. Often the landowner owned the mill, too. Once dressed, Catskill bluestone was used as sidewalks, curbs, door sills, lintels, and building stone. The bluestone here actually is blue, but the sedimentary, hard, fine-grained siltstone comes in brown, red, and gray.

Back on the trail, enjoy a level stretch where red oak mixes into the forest. After the next switchback the soil becomes well drained and the forest composition changes to red oak and mountain laurel. Now comes a long, moderately steep climb along the shoulder of the ridge, where, once again, you hear the traffic sounds wafting up from the valley below.

On the next switchback, midway along the level stretch, watch on your right for a large, flat-topped, sandstone boulder fallen from somewhere above. Here is an excellent example of cross-bedding. Each parallel layer is a solidified sand deposit from an ancient streambed. The boulder is being colonized by lichens and mosses.

In about 2 miles you arrive at Baldwin Memorial lean-to. It is considered good manners to hail a lean-to when approaching even if you suspect no one is home. If you end up having the place to yourself, this is a good spot to sit quietly and watch the local birds foraging and interacting. You can tell what sort of woodsman visited the place before you. A proper user leaves the floor swept. There should be no litter anywhere. The ashes in the fireplace should be clean and clear of trash and half-burnt wood. Neatly stacked, separate piles of firewood and tinder for the next person are stowed dry beneath the front step, and the area between lean-to and fireplace should be clean and orderly. Are the ashes still warm? The Lenape who called the Esopus River Valley home today still maintain a tradition of leaving a fresh-baked cake of cornbread beneath a stone in the ashes for the next camper. There is nothing like having a bite of fresh food and a clean camp when you first arrive worn out from a day's long trek with a heavy pack.

Continue onward and upward through a lovely, dark hemlock stand whose moist slope grows oxalis. Continue onto a shoulder of the mountain and along its crest. There is paper birch here, and black cherry, brambles, and the aroma of bruised hay-scented fern. Grasses dwindle the road to a footpath. The many dead trees have allowed a lot of full sunlight onto the forest floor, and there is considerable dense shrub and sapling growth.

In 2¾ miles you are nearing the summit and encounter the Tremper Mountain lean-to. So few people use this camp that phoebes regularly nest in the crossbeam. Check for them and their staring, horrified fledglings before you enter. Do not disturb them, or they will flop out of their nest to flee you and may get injured. A short distance farther brings you to the summit and the decrepit fire tower. Return the way you came.

The Wittenberg

Location: Woodland Valley
Distance: 6.8 miles
Owner: State of New York

The Wittenberg. Guidebooks from the late 1800s speak of all the high peaks this way: The Slide. The Cornell. The Wittenberg. Only the latter seems to have survived, although its common use is falling away.

Naturalist John Burroughs described the Wittenberg as a "sharp spruce-covered cone." He thought the view from the Wittenberg "more striking" than that from Slide. Personally, I prefer Slide to Wittenberg, because the view extends in more directions, although some might argue that the Wittenberg's ledge is more picturesque and better suited for lounging in the sun. (In winter, the Wittenberg's ledge takes the full force of the icy wind; the chilled hiker barely pauses to notice the view.) From Slide you can see the Wittenberg, but from the Wittenberg you cannot see Slide. I also enjoy the Wittenberg's cap of red spruce and balsam fir. Unlike Slide, the steep ascent up the Wittenberg from Woodland Valley involves some rock scrambling. Wear hiking boots rather than sneakers; you will need the ankle support. If you visit during rain or early in the spring, brooks will abound and the trail will be wet. Like Slide, this is a popular peak. Expect crowds on sunny weekends.

Access

Coming from the east, exit NY 28 into Phoenicia. In 0.1 mile turn left onto High Street. This will loop you beneath the NY 28 overpass. Drive 5.9 miles on Woodland Valley Road to parking on your right just before the ranger station and campground. There is a $3-per-car day-use fee.

Trail

From the parking lot, walk back along the paved road a few yards to the red-marked trailhead on the left. Cross the Woodland Creek on

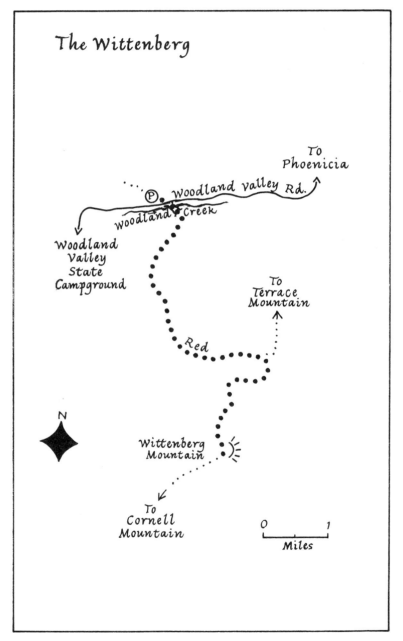

The Wittenberg

a footbridge and begin a steep climb through the northern hardwood, slope community of yellow birch, beech, and sugar maple with some red maple, hemlock, and moosewood. Once out of the ravine, the trail levels off, still climbing but not as steeply. In autumn, the pathway may disappear beneath the fallen red, yellow, and deep gold leaves, or you might wander off among the boulders where the route is unclear. Sight your way from red marker to red marker. Soon you arrive at the first view of Woodland Valley through hemlock trees from a ledge.

Keep on the red trail. At one point it jogs left while an un-marked and abandoned trail continues straight. A pocket of the first red spruces, followed by the first paper birches, heralds the coming transition to boreal woods, but it is only a tease. The trail immediately heads back downhill. Shortly afterward, arrive at a trail junction with a sign. Turn right uphill.

So far, beech has been the principal component of the beech, sugar maple, yellow birch forest. But the higher you climb, the more frequent the incidence of yellow birch. Then hobblebush appears. The height of all the trees lessens. The trail tilts very steeply in places. At one point you climb a sheer rock face using hand- and footholds. This ledge represents an abrupt change in vegetation. On top grow moun-tain-ash, paper birch, balsam fir *(Abies balsamea)*, and red spruce *(Picea rubens)*, all of them stunted by the harshness of the habitat: shallow soil, cold temperatures, a short growing season, lower availability of water and nutrients, and exposure to winds and storms. Ahead through the leafless paper birches in cold months can be seen the summit, topped by dark boreal forest adapted to these difficult growing conditions.

Proceed a bit farther through hardwoods, then enter the boreal woods grown over a talus fall. Distinguish spruce from fir by running your hand along a branch. A spruce will prick your fingers. Its short needles are sharp, pointy, and stiff. Fir needles are flat, flexible, and blunt, longer and more lush than spruce needles. Both fir and spruce needles contain high amounts of tannin, turpentine, and vitamin C. Break a fir needle in half and sniff. Balsam fir is medicinal and highly fragrant. Spruce smells tangier. Both taste strong, practically biting back. The mere aroma of fresh balsam was thought to be virtuous to

At the summit of the Wittenberg, "you are here on the eastern brink of the southern Catskills, and the earth falls away at your feet and curves down through an immense stretch of forest till it joins the plain of Shokan, and thence sweeps away to the Hudson and beyond." — John Burroughs

health. The Catskill Mountain House, along with other inns, once ornamented its halls with balsam boughs for the health of its consumptive guests.

Bowers of red rowan fruit hang over the trail against the dark cloak of evergreen needles. The trail leads steeply through talus and ledge. Pass the 3500-foot-elevation sign, which warns against camping and fires. Paper birch nearly disappears. The forest becomes impenetrable, lush spruce and fir. The smell of balsam permeates the silent air. Listen for juncos, chickadees, and the distinctive "naa, naa" of the red-breasted nuthatch. You might flush grouse. Some of the evergreen spires have been flagged by the prevailing winter winds. The boreal floor grows some mosses and herbs, including the diminutive dogwood bunchberry and goldthread *(Coptis trifola,* formerly *groenlandica).* But there is not so much of these as on Slide, perhaps due to the heavy trampling this mountain suffers.

At the 3780-foot summit cliff, you overlook the Ashokan Reservoir and can tell if the region is drought stricken by the width of the brown perimeter of beach. The plain of Shokan was flooded in 1913 by impounding Esopus Creek. The result, Ashokan Reservoir, is part of New York City's water-supply system. Smog pinkens the air and obscures the view of the Taconics to the east. The Devil's Path of northern Catskill peaks and the escarpment, or edge of the Catskills, stretches to your left. The entire Shawangunk range extends to the south. Ashokan High Point is clearly visible to your far right. Far below, Wittenberg Brook grumbles in the valley floor of Maltby Hollow.

Merlins swoop through the air, hunting small birds and large insects. These are falcons, with long, pointed wings and long tails. Merlins are larger than the common kestrel and smaller than the endangered peregrine falcon; altogether they are a bit larger than a blue jay. Merlin is the falcon of the summer boreal woods and breeds only in the spruce-fir forest.

Leave the ledge and stroll along the trail toward Cornell Mountain for a short way. Explore the silent, dark-needled boreal forest. The air temperature stays cooler here than on the slopes and in the valleys in all seasons. A succulent mattress of mosses and lichens coats the ground.

Return back the way you came. I always leave the boreal woods with a pang of sadness. It takes so much work to get up here into the northern forest. As you descend, watch the change from spruce and fir to paper birch, and then to yellow birch and beech, followed by sugar maple, yellow birch, and beech, and, finally, hemlock at the very end. The lower slope forest resounds with the squeaks of katydids by late afternoon as you trek a forest thrown into shadow by the sun setting behind the mountain's shoulder.

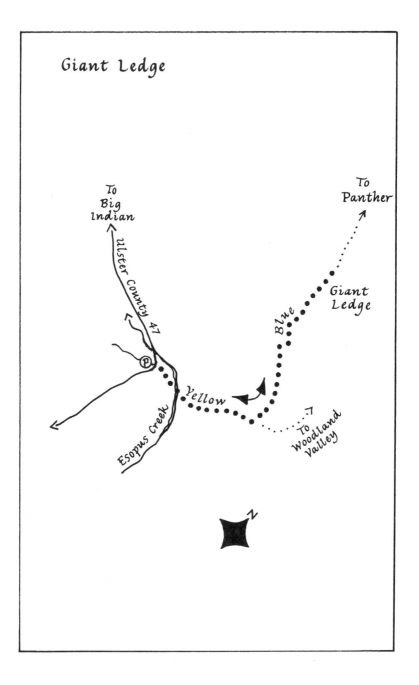

Giant Ledge

To
Big
Indian

Ulster County 47

To
Panther

P

Blue

Giant
Ledge

Yellow

To
Woodland
Valley

Esopus Creek

N

Giant Ledge

Location: Oliverea
Distance: 3.2 miles
Owner: State of New York

Giant Ledge is actually a series of ledges between Panther and Slide Mountains. In winter, the short slog through treacherous snow and ice—short compared to hikes elsewhere—rewards the walker with a grand view. In spring, the pink wild azaleas and northern wildflowers bloom. In summer, you can laze upon the heated rocks wishing for the humid haze to clear. In fall, there are few more accessible sites for a vast panorama of golden hills. This is a popular place. Expect company, especially on weekends. You may tent camp on top of the ledges so long as you are out of sight of the trail. This is *the* place to come for sunrises.

Access

From the intersection of NY 28 and NY 42 in Shandaken, proceed west on NY 28. Just before Big Indian, turn left at the sign for Big Indian–Oliverea Valley onto Ulster County 47, also called Oliverea–Slide Mountain Road. Go 7.5 miles to marked parking at a hairpin turn.

Trail

The yellow-marked trail traverses the bright and open, northern hardwood, slope forest community of sugar maple, yellow birch, and beech with some red maple, the shrub layer composed of sapling trees and moosewood, the herb layer lush with ferns. Sign in at the trail register just before the brook. This tiny water is the beginning of the mighty Esopus Creek. Shortly, the trail begins its steep climb.

Oxalis or wood-sorrel *(Oxalis montana;* Europe retains the old name *O. acetosella)* grows among shining club moss. In ancient Ireland this worldwide species was called the shamrock. Each night the three sour-tasting leaflets fold; they open again next morning. It is the boreal cousin of the "sour clover" or yellow wood-sorrel kids snack on in lowland backyards and waste places.

Turn left onto the blue-marked trail at the intersection in the saddle between Giant Ledge and Slide Mountain. The road continues with some moderate and gentle climbing, then a short but steep climb through a talus fall past sugar maples and black cherry. Rock tripe lichen encrusts the bedrock outcrops.

The summit, with its abrupt change to stunted trees, is actually a col between Panther and Slide Mountains. The marked trail heads left, but you can explore the side trails to your right that lead along the string of cliff edges. There are views of Woodland Valley, Wittenberg, Cornell, and a slope of Slide Mountain. On a clear day you can see the northern Catskills.

As you walk, survey the plants. There is a lot of black cherry (an important subsidiary, Catskill forest component above 3000 feet) and black raspberry among the stunted, enchanting yellow birch and beech. And at 3400 feet Giant Ledge supports a tantalizing array of northern species that introduces the visitor to what it must be like in the boreal stands that occur in the Catskills above 3500 feet. Find a token representation of balsam fir, red spruce, and hobblebush. Mountain-ash *(Sorbus americana)* or rowan is a small tree or shrub that bears flat-topped clusters of white flowers. These ripen into sour red berries so heavy they cause the stems to droop. Many birds and mammals eat them, and I hear some people boil them into jam. Bunchberry *(Cornus canadensis)* is a dwarf dogwood tree no higher than 8 inches. The flower is reminiscent of the flowering dogwood of the lowlands, although I find the bunchberry bracts seem a purer white and are arranged more crisply in an exact, tight square around the yellow-green flowers in the center. A drift of these abloom in June looks like snow; however, too few grow (perhaps I should say survive, considering the amount of trampling and abuse by human visitors) on Giant Ledge for this effect. The flowers mature into a cluster of red dogwood berries with stony seeds, which gives rise to the name bunchberry. Clintonia (*Clintonia borealis,* in the north known as corn lily), early azalea *(Rhododendron rosea),* Canada mayflower, and

The view of Woodland Valley from Giant Ledge

starflower *(Trientalis borealis)* bloom around Memorial Day. Witch-hazel, lowbush blueberry, huckleberry, trillium, sarsaparilla, large-leaved goldenrod, and goldthread also grow here. Great mossy boulders lie in the woods. Some sport black rock tripe lichens big as bats. Lie on your belly on one of the ledges to peer over the edge at the talus beneath. Pin cherry scrabbles along the face of the cliffs, along with paper birch. Some of these birches with the peeling white bark are actually a local, high-altitude subspecies with heart-shaped leaves called round-leaved or mountain white birch *(Betula cordifolia).*

If you brought overnight supplies you may camp on Giant Ledge, so long as you are not visible from the main trail. Arise from your tent at dawn to sit on the ledges; they face straight east into the sunrise. Some mornings come clear and the gentle colors of the sky are pure and clean. Other mornings, cloud fills Woodland Valley below, isolating Giant Ledge above within a glow of new pink sunlight. If you do camp at Giant Ledge, a good day hike is up Panther Mountain. The return trip leads back the way you came.

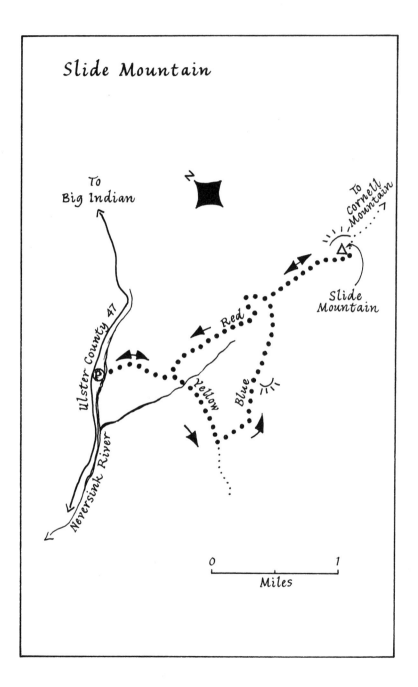

Slide Mountain

To
Big Indian

To
Cornell
Mountain

Slide
Mountain

Red

Yellow

Blue

Ulster County 47

Neversink River

N

0   1
         Miles

Slide Mountain

Location: Oliverea
Distance: 7 miles
Owner: State of New York

S lide Mountain, the highest peak in the Catskills, is capped with a balsam fir boreal forest and spectacular views.

Access
From Big Indian, drive 9.5 miles south on Ulster County 47/Oliverea–Slide Mountain Road. There is marked parking on your left.

Trail
This way to the top is a little longer than others, but it is more interesting, less traveled, and in better condition. You will need a full day for this walk. Be prepared for sudden bad weather. Carry warm clothes even in summer.

The yellow-marked trail crosses one branch of the West Branch of the newborn Neversink on steppingstones of boulders, and heads into the open Catskill woods of yellow birch, sugar maple, and beech with some red maple. Cross a brook or two, depending on the wetness of the season, and begin the climb.

The trail jogs right onto an old, level road that follows along the slope. Keep straight past the popular red-marked trail turnoff for Slide Mountain. Cross the other tributary to the West Branch of the Neversink on a footbridge. A large amount of hobblebush grows on both banks. My favorite part of hobblebush is its leaf buds. These look like they are dusted with gold. Use a magnifying glass to appreciate the golden hairs on the stems, shoots, and opening leaves, arranged like tiny, metallic star-bursts. When the leaf buds first break open in late April, they look like little tapered and crinkled golden cups.

October snow squalls blow across the golden autumn Catskill hills framed by the stiff limbs of the marvelous balsam fir (Abies balsamea) *atop Slide Mountain.*

Soon after the hobblebush brook, you arrive at a fork. Keep left uphill on the yellow trail. This will bring you to a level saddle between hills. Turn left onto the blue-marked trail for the 2.25-mile climb up Slide Mountain. You have come about halfway. The circa-1800 granite monument pillar here informs you that you have stepped onto the Curtis and Ormsbee Trail.

At rock outcrops you encounter the boreal plant species: mountain-ash, balsam fir, paper birch, and bunchberry. Boreal simply means something from the north, named for Boreas, Greek god of the cold, blowing north wind. The highest peaks of the Catskills extend to an altitude where temperature, storm exposure, water availability, and soil depth are identical to more northern conditions. Visitors get a taste of the taiga—the northern coniferous forest—of Canada.

Climb into thick balsam fir *(Abies balsamea)* woods mixed with paper birch. The change is arresting. Listen for the calls of juncos and the whirring "cheee" of cedar waxwings. The trail levels and the beautiful and dark balsam disappears, to be replaced by mixed hardwoods. This pattern repeats itself several times. At the next north-facing ledge, where environmental conditions are harsher (read *boreal*), grow the balsam fir, mountain-ash, and paper birch. Waxwings flush out of the thick branches as you survey the wide views. Once you leave the ledge for the more protected and milder slope, the forest turns back into the northern hardwood stand. Pass the sign that announces 3500 feet above sea level. Above this height you may not camp, a restriction that protects the fragile plants and soil from trampling and erosion. At the third outcrop, take the side trail to your right through damp sphagnum that smells of peat. This brings you to a view. Neversink Valley extends west and south. To the right of that are Wildcat, Hemlock, Spruce, Fir, Big Indian, Table, and Doubletop Mountains, followed by the Beaver Kill Range. The highest hills are topped by boreal forest.

Continue your climb up a slope covered in an enchanting forest of silvery yellow birch and beech. The trail bed is made up of sand and rounded pink, white, and gray quartz pebbles. These are the weathered remains of the strong and coarse sandstone conglomerate that caps the Catskill escarpment and preserves its softer shale layers beneath. It is the reason why the Catskill High Peaks seem to be of a height, capped by the same, resistant layer. A thin layer of dark, nutrient-poor humus seen on the trail verge is all that covers the rock and all that supports the boreal woods. Balsam fir forest can survive on 3-inch-deep soil, whereas yellow birch requires 9 inches; red oak, 18 inches; and sugar maple, 2 feet. The cold and acidity from fallen fir needles inhibit bacterial activity and therefore decay, so soil development is slowed or may hardly occur here at all.

At the red trail, turn right for the half-mile tramp to the summit. Gradually the gradient rises as you follow a ridge edge whose crest falls away on either side of the trail. Watch for scales of fir cones on the ground left by red squirrel. You may also see other eaters of fir seeds: crossbills, purple finches, and evening grosbeaks.

The first opening just before the summit offers a fine view. There are Ashokan Reservoir, Cornell, Wittenberg, Panther, and a small cliff on an insignificant saddle that is Giant Ledge. And there is—wait a minute, where did the view go? How could fog come in so fast? Suddenly it feels so cold. It's starting to sleet. Ah, there, the clouds have flown apart, what a view! And now it's shrouded again. Climbers of high peaks are familiar with this unpredictable and often deadly weather change.

The summit view is obscured partially by the forest. Here once stood two lean-tos and an observation tower. You are standing on the Catskill Divide. Rain or snow falling on the south and west side of this clearing flows into the Neversink tributaries and ultimately into the Delaware River (see chapter 9, "Delaware River Heritage Trail"). Precipitation that falls on the north side of the clearing flows into Esopus Creek and ultimately into the Hudson River (see chapter 24, "Ruth Reynolds Glunt Nature Preserve"). Continue on the trail downhill to a ledge overlook ornamented with a plaque to John Burroughs, where spreads a vast panorama of 70 Catskill peaks, the Hudson Valley, the Shawangunks, the Hudson Highlands, east to the Taconics, the Berkshires, and the Green Mountains (on a clear day), and south to New Jersey and Pennsylvania. To give you an idea of how vast the view is, read Van Loan's *Catskill Mountain Guide* of 1879. The description of the view from Slide, naming the mountains, valleys, and distant ranges, goes on for two pages, and still does not describe everything.

So where is the 1820 landslide that gave the mountain its name? If you were to push through the balsam toward Woodland Valley, you would without warning find yourself on the brink of the scree overgrown with trees. Please don't do it. The trampling of such a bushwhack does tremendous damage to the soil and plants, and there is really nothing to see.

The impenetrable balsam fir hardly stirs under the blasts of wind. Sit for a while in the damp, silent darkness where grow only mosses and the shining evergreen leaves of goldthread. It is possible, even probable, to run into porcupines on Slide Mountain any time of the year. If you want to be assured of a run-in, camp overnight in the saddle between Slide and Cornell (carry water). Don't leave unattended on the ground any piece of equipment you really like.

Return the way you came, this time keeping straight on the red trail toward Winnisook. Soon comes the transition to mountain-ash and yellow birch. Descend farther into beech woods. All along you see less and less balsam fir, until it totally disappears before the 3500-foot sign. This jeep road is washed out and the rocky descent is steep. If the time has gone on toward evening, in summer stop and stand still to hear the thrushes singing; in spring, listen to the grouse drumming. I grew up on the east bank of the Hudson River. The thrushes sing differently here on Slide Mountain, a varying dialect of the same song. At the bottom, turn right on the old town road, and then left to descend to the parking lot.

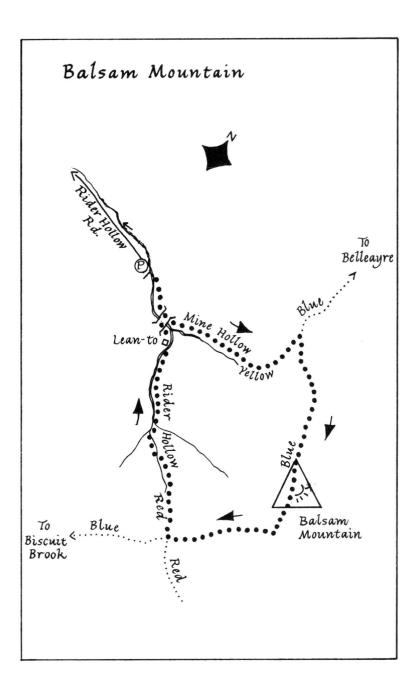

Balsam Mountain

N

Rider Hollow Rd.

P

To Belleayre

Blue

Mine Hollow

Lean-to

Yellow

Rider Hollow

Blue

Red

Balsam Mountain

To Biscuit Brook

Blue

Red

Balsam Mountain

Location: Mapledale/Rider Hollow
Distance: 5 miles
Owner: State of New York

This climb to the summit of Balsam Mountain involves a loop through the Big Indian–Beaverkill Range Wilderness along the Rider Hollow and Mine Hollow Trails. There is only a small and limited view from the summit. The attraction of the area is that it is seldom used. Trails are narrow, primeval, and enchanting. The place seems untouched, and the forest stands silent except for birdsong and wind.

You can tent overnight at the designated site within the spruce plantation right at the trailhead, perhaps feeling guilty, as I did, to trample the carpet of blooming oxalis and Canada mayflower. Or you can take your chances at finding room at the lean-to half a mile in from the parking lot. Either way, you can then arise the next morning for an early start. However, this is not necessary, as this is only a half-day hike. But there is nothing like seeing the rising sunshine slant through the spruces onto the sword-groves of ferns, or at evening when the setting sun casts dusty shadows across the gold-shot water of the mossy brook.

Access

From Pine Hill, drive west along US 28 to the top of the hill at Highmount. Turn left at the sign for Belleayre Mountain Ski Center onto Ulster County 49A. Drive 5.1 miles to a left onto Rider Hollow Road. Drive 2.2 miles to parking at the dead end.

Trail

Walk around the gate onto the red-marked trail and sign in at the register box. Right off, you are struck by the wildness of the place. It is shady, cool, moist, and lush. A clear and cold stream gurgles beneath hemlocks. Small and supple trout zoom among the mossy rocks of the deep pools. Oxalis mounds over the forest floor, except where crowded aside by thick and glossy Canada mayflower. Corn lily, foamflower *(Tiarella cordifolia)*, and Virginia waterleaf *(Hydrophyllum virginianum)* grow in abundance in the rich soil.

Follow the brook upstream along the old woods road. Cross the brook on steppingstones. Watch for scarlet tanager along this stretch of brook.

Arrive at a sunny opening. There used to be a lean-to here, but vandals burned it in 1994. Do not cross the bridge. That is your return route. Bear left onto the yellow-marked Mine Hollow Trail. On your left rises the beech and hemlock slope. On your right stand the lush brookside sugar maple and yellow birch. Find pink pyrola *(Pyrola asarifolia)* and shinleaf *(P. ellyptica)*. This is a place to fall under the enchantment of the greenwood. The narrow trail wends its way along the purling brook grown up in jewelweed. Pluck a leaf and hold it underwater to see its silver foil, which will surface perfectly dry. The veery sings its water-thrush song, spilling silver into the green in a waterfall of tumbling notes. Where the stream forks, the trail follows a tributary. Watch for trillium in spring. Across the bank rises a stunning hemlock woods. A sweet smell permeates the ravine.

The hollow deepens into a crease as the trail slants steeply along the bright beech bank accompanied by sugar maple, hemlock, yellow birch and a few basswood, elm, black cherry, and groves of hay-scented fern. The only sounds you hear are birdsong and that deep, empty sound the wind makes over a great expanse of forest. The path switchbacks and then runs steeply straight up out of the hollow past one of the most beautiful towering hemlock forests I have ever seen. Watch for hepatica in early spring. Pass around boulders of striated stream deposits as you near the crest of the level col between Belleayre and Balsam Mountains. Turn right onto the blue-marked trail. You have come halfway to the summit.

Pass beech, sugar maple, and yellow birch. Here and there find moosewood (you saw this lower down, too) and seedlings of mountain-ash. Beneath the trees spread acres of hay-scented fern. You hardly need to crush the lacy leaves for the smell; warm sunlight

In early July, the fairy cups of oxalis bloom above the green shamrock leaves.
Five long, white petals as thin as onionskin paper are striped with magenta.
In the center, glowing magenta circles the white corolla. The base of each
petal is marked with a yellow spot.

evaporates the volatile oil onto the summer air and scents the breeze. An aggressive species, hay-scented fern can hold control of a place for decades, crowding out other plants.

Within about 30 feet you will find a patch of wild oats, or sessile bellwort *(Uvularia sessilifolia),* on your right. Traverse the level col. Ahead you can see high Balsam Mountain. As you climb, yellow birch and black cherry displace the beech and sugar maple. Moosewood and mountain-ash now attain tree height. You start to see scraggly balsam fir outlying the main population. Beside the hay-scented fern you will see another fern, one with a blue tint to its green, always growing in shade. This is mountain woodfern *(Dryopteris campyloptera,* formerly *austriaca),* used commercially by florists. You may put up a ruffed grouse or two as the forest of silvery yellow birch becomes stunted and twisted. Pass the 3500-foot elevation sign. Polypody ferns cap boulders.

The long, level summit woods—mostly on private land—are

open, sunny groves of hay-scented fern and mountain woodfern interspersed with statuesque and symmetrical specimens of glossy, black-needled balsam fir and short black cherry, yellow birch, mountain-ash, and hobblebush. On days of low clouds, mist washes through the trees and fingers the fern meadows. Balsam Mountain is 3600 feet high, only just above the growing elevation of balsam fir, so the conifers are not so thick here as they are on top of Slide or Balsam Lake Mountain. The fir seems to grow most plentifully where environmental conditions are harshest: along the north edge of the summit and at summit ledges. Black cherry has proven to be the leading dominant species of this site. Robert McIntosh, in his *The Forests of the Catskill Mountains,* suggests that this summit may have been wind devastated or burned, so perhaps in the past there was more fir or even spruce. The dense fern groves inhibit the establishment of fir seedlings.

In winter there are views through the trees, but in summer you must keep on across the level summit until you reach a small cutaway view on your left. This is a good place to rest and gaze at the steep slope that plunges into Lost Clove and Indian Hollow. There is no birdsong up here, except, perhaps, from a flock of chickadees. Faraway screams of blue jay packs and veery waterfalls drift up on the air from below, along with sounds from the village of Big Indian and US 28.

As you begin your descent, the groves of hay-scented fern contain false hellebore *(Veratrum viride),* also called Indian poke. About 4 feet tall here, but capable of attaining 6 feet, this plant contains powerful alkaloids used as a respiratory and cardiac depressant and as an insecticide. So strong is its poison that a comb rinsed in hellebore root tea and drawn through the hair will kill head lice.

The trail drops steeply downhill into the realm of sugar maple and birdsong. At the crossroads, turn right onto the red-marked Rider Hollow Trail for the 1.7-mile jaunt to the parking lot.

Dry Brook

Location: Seager
Distance: 4 miles
Owner: Private and State of New York

On some days the walker strives for views and justifies a hike only if it rewards with a panorama from a mountaintop. This walk is for those other days, when you yearn for the silence of deep forests. The remote and seldom-used Seager trailhead leads for nearly 3 miles along privately owned Dry Brook before it reaches state land on Shandaken Brook in the Big Indian Wilderness. There are waterfalls and the chance to see wildlife. The Dry Brook valley was once a big bear-hunting area.

There are no footbridges across the many brook fords, so you may get your feet wet, especially in spring or after prolonged rain. I recommend you wear long pants in summer, due to all the stinging nettles that line the path.

Ranger Charles Platt explains that "Dry Brook" is a bastardization of the German *drei,* which means "three," a reference to the three historic covered bridges whose reproductions you see on the drive along the valley.

Access

From Pine Hill, motor west on US 28 to the top of the hill at Highmount. Turn left at the big sign for Belleayre Mountain Ski Center onto Ulster County 49A. Drive 5.6 miles. Turn left onto Ulster County 49 (Dry Brook Road). Follow this for 4.3 miles, past all side roads and driveways, keeping straight on the main road. You will pass three covered bridges. The first sits on the site of the Forge, where once iron ore for smelting was imported (all the way) from Hudson Valley mines. It seems that Dry Brook provided good waterpower for this process. Pig iron was shipped back out of the Forge for sale in New York City. Follow deeper into the hills as the road narrows from

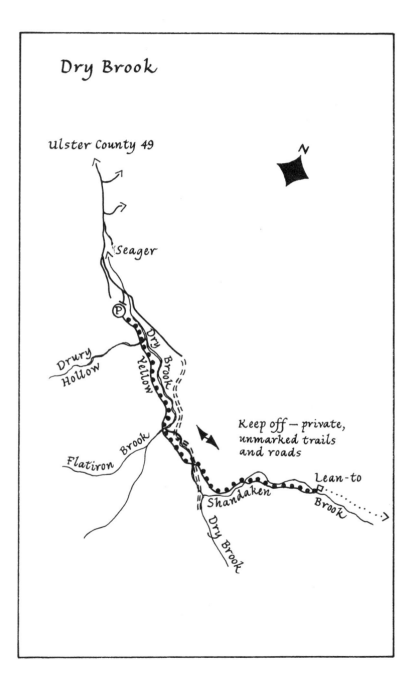

Dry Brook

Ulster County 49

Seager

Drury Hollow

Dry Brook

Yellow

Flatiron Brook

Keep off — private, unmarked trails and roads

Shandaken Brook

Lean-to

Dry Brook

pavement to gravel, and finally to dirt. Toward the end there is a confusing fork. Keep straight (do not cross the covered bridge) to the parking area at the road's dead end.

Trail

Clear, cold Dry Brook laughs and ripples. When summertime heat and lack of rainfall drop the water level, European coltsfoot—the old-time remedy for sore throats and coughs—overgrows the exposed cobbles. The yellow-marked old woods road leads past streamside hemlocks and yellow birch mixed with sugar maple and beech. Where the road fords the creek, the yellow trail keeps straight along the bank.

Follow the markers across the seasonal stream that in spring drains Drury Hollow. By summer this cascade always dries up. Pass through several wet areas of false nettle *(Boehmeria cylindrica)*, wood nettle *(Laportea canadensis)*, celery-scented cow parsnip *(Heracleum maximum,* formerly *H. lanatum)*, and tall meadow rue *(Thalyctrum pubescens,* formerly *polygamum)*. It is important to learn the difference between false and true nettles if you want to save yourself some discomfort. The surest way would be to touch both, but I do not recommend this! Stinging nettle leaves and stems are lined with hypodermic stinging hairs that really smart with the slightest brushing touch. The bristles are apparent. Wood nettle does not smart as sharply. False nettle, also called bog-hemp, looks just like a stinging nettle without the hairs. Native Peoples throughout the Americas know that every plant poisonous to humans grows its companion antidote nearby; you only have to know what it is to look for it. Should *you* get stung, find some of the tall dock that grows nearby. Mash a leaf and apply immediately to the stung area. If you cannot find any dock, then slit a stem of jewelweed and apply its juice.

I was passing through one of these cow parsnip–nettle patches when I heard a rustling and saw an adult black bear turning around a scant 20 feet away. It ran up the hemlock slope and, when I followed, I saw it had used a well-trodden path that led up out of sight in one direction; in the other, it passed through the cow parsnip headed for the creek. Bears use regular paths. I found a few crossing

The lean-to on Shandaken Brook. Ruttenbur translated Shandaken *as "at the hemlock woods" or "place of hemlocks," a reference to what once grew here.*

perpendicular to the human path. You can tell them from deer paths because the bear pads sink indentations without the mark of sharp edges of hooves. Bear prints can turn up the soil, and the vegetation alongside is usually bent or broken. Dry Brook runs in the heart of the southern-central Catskills, at the end of a dead-end road, buffered on all sides from the outside world by the Beaverkill Range, Mill Brook Ridge, Dry Brook Ridge, and the Catskill Divide. What better place to see bears? But I only saw one because I was in the right place at the right time, alone and traveling quietly, and the woods were deserted of other humans. Bears have poor vision and only moderate hearing. They sense things mostly through their noses. Black bears are normally nocturnal, but I have seen them now and then at midday. When you see one for the first time, it will look for all the world like a big dog.

The road returns and follows the foot of the hollow wall. Oxalis grows in carpets across the floor, and there is an abundance of cornflower. Arrive at a waterfall that sluices through a path of green mosses into a bedrock slab pool of turquoise water. Flatiron Brook cascades into Dry Brook. In springtime, Ranger Platt says he has sometimes had to turn back at this point, unable to ford Flatiron Brook. Go a bit farther and the road intersects with a well-used private road at a bridge over more enchanting waterfalls. Keep straight, following the yellow markers. You are now halfway to the lean-to.

Where the road fords the creek, you keep straight on the yellow path to the trail's own ford. If you have somehow managed to keep your feet dry, you might get them wet now. This is where the dry-foots show their color. "Dry-foot" hikers will go to any length to keep their hiking boots dry, while "wet-foot" hikers jump right into the first puddle they feel they cannot avoid.

Follow the yellow path across the road and into the bright beech woods with an undergrowth of hay-scented fern. This grassy road cuts up and across the slope that separates Dry Brook from Shandaken Brook. Pass the sound of more waterfalls in the hemlocks darkening Shandaken Brook. The path leads along a wet slope of grasses, sedges, jewelweed, and ferns. Cross a brook. The path leads deeper and deeper into wilderness where there is not another living soul (at least not on weekdays).

Enter state land and designated wilderness. Sign in at the register box. Pass through the tall woods of sugar maple, yellow birch, black cherry, and ash, and shortly arrive at the lean-to. Here is a pipe with clean groundwater. The sturdy lean-to sports a low roof and a partial wall in the front for cold-weather camping. If you continue on the trail, you will climb the col between Eagle and Big Indian Mountains, meeting up with the blue-marked trail that runs for 14 miles from Belleayre to Biscuit Brook, known as the Pine Hill–West Branch Trail.

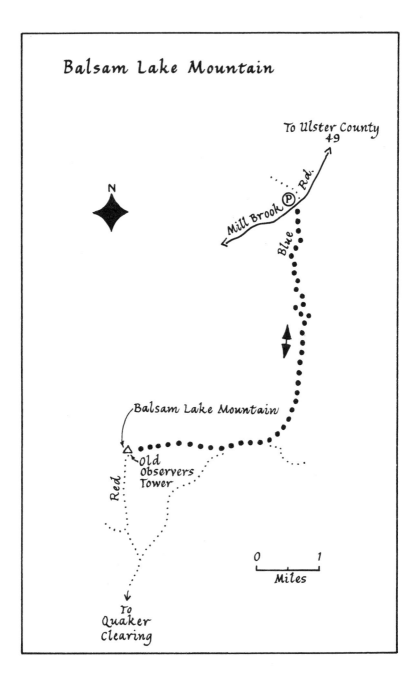

Balsam Lake
Mountain

Location: Hardenbergh
Distance: 6 miles
Owner: Private and State of New York

This is *the* mountain to climb for views of the Catskills, if you are willing to negotiate a tricky fire tower. The first level of stairs has been removed. However, plans call for a new tower staffed with an observer or a summit steward. Balsam Lake Mountain was the site of New York State's first fire tower. This mountain's slanted level summit is capped with a thicket of balsam fir.

The trail uses the fire tower observer's jeep road. For most of its length the way traverses private land. Hikers can cross this property so long as they keep to the trail. Not until you near the summit do you enter state land. The first 2 miles of walking is easy to moderate, which saves the stiff climb for the summit.

Access

From US 28 at Highmount just west of Pine Hill, turn left onto Ulster County 49A and drive 5.5 miles to a left onto Ulster County 49. Go 1.4 miles. At the fork where there is a road maintenance shed in the center of the triangle called "Millbrook," bear right onto Mill Brook Road. Go 2.3 miles to the top of the hill. Parking is on your right.

Trail

Walk across Mill Brook Road up to the top of the hill and find the unmarked trailhead for the blue jeep road that leads into the woods. (The trail you see at the parking lot heads north over Dry Brook Ridge to Arkville. Do not go that way.) Sign in at the register box and begin the long, moderate-to-level climb through northern hardwood forest.

In about 2 miles the road forks. Bear right on the red-marked trail and enter state land. As you climb you will begin to see in boulders and outcrops the conglomerate bedrock that caps the highest peaks of the Catskills. The top of this first rise brings you to state land. Now the forest is made up of stunted yellow birch, black cherry, and balsam fir, with mountain-ash, moosewood, hay-scented fern, and oxalis. Red maple and beech only occur in small elfin groves or in areas protected from the elements. Sedges crop up wherever it is wet and sunny.

Pass the 3500-foot elevation mark. Two short and steep climbs bring you to groves of hay-scented fern waving among the trees. It looks like the summit of Balsam Mountain, but you are not yet to the summit of Balsam Lake Mountain.

The top is elusive. With each steep climb followed by a level run, you think you are at the top, only to be faced with yet another steep pitch. Summer sun evaporates the smell of balsam into the air. The woods become predominately fir and the tower comes into view. It looks like the spruce-fir woods of the Adirondacks or of Nova Scotia (minus the spruce). Find fire cherry, mountain holly, corn lily, bunchberry, and goldthread. The ruins are the old observer's building.

When I questioned a local ranger closely about this tower, he reassured me one could still climb up as far as the cab floor even though the first set of stairs is gone. I managed to haul myself up the frame, envious of a group of youths who came after me and lifted themselves onto the first landing in half-a-second easy as chocolate. If there were no fire tower here, you would get only a peek at views. Climb up and you will get a 360-degree, unforgettable panorama. Just please be careful. Parts of the tower are already missing and its condition will only worsen with time. If a new tower is in place, the point is moot.

Looking east back over the trail you walked, find the distinctive sloping shape of Slide Mountain in the space between Doubletop and nearby Graham Mountain. The mountain scarred by ski trails is Belleayre. To the west runs Mill Brook Ridge. To the south is the Beaverkill Range; to the north is Dry Brook Ridge. And there are many, many more. The whole view is made up of mountains and deep and wide valleys between hills. Many people feel that this is the best view from a fire tower in all the Catskills.

While you are up here, take a look at the spires of the balsam fir canopy. In summer you should be able to see the upright, fleshy cones forming. There is usually a lot of bird activity in these spires. In summer, foraging chickadees, warblers, and slate-colored juncos flit from spire to spire. Also in summer, white-throated sparrows sing "old Sam Peabody, Peabody, Peabody" in their clear voices. This activity in the spires is not apparent when you stand on the ground. Lowlanders may be entranced by the juncos and sparrows, normally only seen and heard in the dead of winter. These birds summer in boreal forests.

From the tower, survey the dense balsam fir stand of the summit. Patches where the firs seem stunted or younger, populated with dead, silvery fir trunks, underlain with lighter green, are wet basins in the bedrock grown up in sphagnum moss into balsam fir bog. In the Catskills this is a rarity and a cherished natural system. But farther north, in the Adirondack and Canadian spruce-fir woods, it is normal. The northern conifer forest typically grows over a shallow soil, moist due to the level bedrock that traps and holds water. Sphagnum moss rooted since shortly after the last glacial epoch has formed layers of moisture-holding peat, creating a dark, spongy, musky-smelling soil infiltrated by the shallow roots of firs susceptible to blowdown.

Once you've climbed down, secrete yourself beside the impenetrable balsam and make the spishing call. The birds will wing for you. The chickadee that is not a chickadee is the black-poll warbler, which is supposed to breed within stunted mountaintop spruce stands but seems right at home here among the stunted firs. Wind in the firs sounds like hollow winter, unlike the soft rippling through deciduous leaves that flap and rustle together.

You might try carefully bushwhacking into the fir stand a way. It is very thick. Hobblebush and piercing dead fir limbs can trap you. Follow the example of deer and bear paths, bending beneath limbs rather than breaking them, avoiding plants by stepping neatly beside them. You might encounter the bright green sphagnum or you might instead find a pool of dazzling white sunlight on the black-needled floor. Some people find boreal forests monotonous. They are. The farther north you travel, the more the ecosystems simplify as species diversity drops.

The red-marked trail continues downhill to a lean-to and then onward to the blue trail downhill toward Quaker Clearing. The return from the summit, however, is back the way you came. As you descend, there are partial views through the trail corridor opening.

Kelly Hollow

Location: Mill Brook Ridge
Distance: 3.8 miles
Owner: State of New York

Kelly Hollow's deep-forested walls slant uphill into the flanks of Mill Brook Ridge. The trailhead lies in Delaware County. The bulk of the trail itself is in Ulster County. There are two loops used for hiking in summer and cross-country skiing in winter, originally farm roads. The shorter is 1.9 miles long. This chapter describes the longer loop.

Kelly Hollow was purchased in the 1920s and 1930s. The Civilian Conservation Corps in the 1930s and 1940s planted the largest stand of Norway spruce I have ever seen in America. I think there is more Norway spruce here than in all of Norway. The hollow has always enjoyed infrequent use. The state has simply left it alone since it was reforested, and it now has gone wild. If you are looking for peace, quiet, and solitude in spruce halls, come here. You can backpack overnight supplies in to the lean-to on the old beaver pond at the head of the hollow, or car camp at the trailheads.

Access

From US 28 at Highmount just west of Pine Hill, turn left onto Ulster County 49A and drive 5.5 miles to a left onto Ulster County 49. Go 1.4 miles. At the fork where there is a road maintenance shed called "Millbrook" in the center of the triangle, bear right onto Mill Brook Road. Go 6.9 miles. The entrance will be on your left.

Trail

From the parking lot, head into the plantation of red pine *(Pinus resinosa)* and Norway spruce *(Picea abies)*, left across a stream, and then onto an old woods road. Within 30 feet of climbing the first rise, look by the brookside for a barn and round silo foundation. In summer it gets so overgrown it becomes hidden. The bank you stand on is

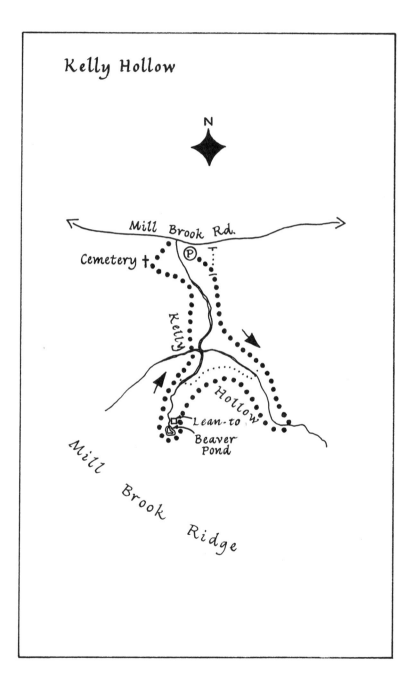

actually hand-built of stone. This is the second-story bridge that you can still see being used on existing old barns as you drive the country lanes of Hardenburgh and the surrounding towns. It gave access to the midstory of the barn between the cattle floor below and the hayloft above. Building into a bank, or making a bank, so that two floors of a three-story structure have access from the ground is an old northern European barn style.

Walk the grassy road past woods of sugar maple, yellow birch, and black cherry. Sign in at the trail register. The road parallels the main stream as you enter hemlocks. The going is moderately uphill. Soon you encounter the left fork for the short loop. If you are in for the whole walk, keep left past the Norway spruce plantation on your left and natural, wild hemlocks on your right.

In Norway, Norway spruce shares the northern forest with other wild species and looks much like our native spruces in America: ragged, untamed, dark. But bring Norway spruce to America, plant it in the full sunlight of abandoned pastures or, better yet, as an ornamental specimen on a front lawn, and the species becomes a statuesque, horticultural shade tree with bold and sweeping limbs. Funny, the way plant and animal species change their habits when placed in a new environment. Unlike those of American spruce species, Norway spruce branchlets hang downward and swing in a breeze.

The spruces are all the same age. They display a common girth and height. The lower limbs are dead from lack of sunlight (perfectly natural and healthy; you can see the same on the hemlocks opposite). They are evenly spaced in their planted rows. Yet the overall effect is not of regimentation. Rather, Kelly Hollow's plantations look like the storybook forests of old fairy tales. They create a silent and dark, tall-standing wood, trunks creaking in a wind and boughs sighing the breathy, spacious moan of otherworldly voices.

In summertime you may find large green cones on the forest floor. Make the spishing call. Red squirrel will answer with furious chatter. This rodent nips free the developing cones and lets them drop. When enough are scattered about on the ground, the animal comes down out of the trees and one by one carries each cone to its favorite perch at the foot of a spruce. Rapidly, the sharp incisors rip the scales aside to reveal the seeds. These it bites off the wing and eats. Scale after scale gets shredded until all that remains is the naked stalk, which gets discarded. Sitting like this at the favorite perch can create a mountain of scales and stalks known as a squirrel midden. Middens that have accumulated for years can grow into substantial piles. I could have sat on the larger middens I saw here as on a throne while nibbling my own lunch.

The road swings out of the plantation while the spruces continue up the hollow out of sight. Follow the ravine wall at a height along a path through deciduous woods. Find pink pyrola, jack-in-the-pulpit, nettle, wild oats, oxalis, round-leaved orchis *(Platanthera orbiculata,* formerly *Habenaria),* wild sarsaparilla, and lycopodiums, also known as club mosses. The trail angles upward to the lean-to nestled beneath magnificent spruces beside a pond. Studies in central New York found that over 100 species of birds use beaver ponds, in addition to otter, mink, muskrat, and numerous amphibians, reptiles, insects, crustaceans, mollusks, and fish. The way to tell if the beaver pond is active is to inspect the lodge and dam. An active site will be freshly plastered with mud. Inactive sites start to get overgrown with plants, something a beaver never permits. The trail circles the pond to your left, but I walked over the dam. A stone foundation forms its base. All the beaver did was cap this by a foot or so, which raised the pond's water level and forced the beaver to extend the dam many yards to one side. Standing hemlocks along the outlet bear old gnaw marks.

Walk along the pond edge. From its downhill side you can see how the pond lies cupped within an amphitheater in the Mill Brook Ridge wall. You can also see the stately posture of the Norway spruces.

Head down the hollow through the woods of sugar maple and ash with a little yellow birch and beech alternated by stands of hemlock. Pass the intersection with the shorter loop and emerge at the end of the hollow beside an old cemetery that is still used by local residents for burials. The town of Middletown maintains the plots. Many graves hold the remains of the original European settlers of the area, including the grave of a Revolutionary War soldier. The earliest date that is legible is from the 1860s. Some of the stones are carved with the Victorian-era motif of shaking hands, symbolizing the meeting of this world with the next. Walk through the conifer plantation and campground following the ski markers to the parking lot.

Alder Lake

Location: Turnwood
Distance: 1.5 miles
Owner: State of New York

I f you are a family looking for a quiet pond on which to tent camp, fish, swim, and relax, come to Alder Lake. There are no facilities other than the lake and the camping sites, so whatever you need for your stay you must bring yourself.

Access

From US 28 at Highmount just west of Pine Hill, turn left onto Ulster County 49A and drive 5.5 miles to a left onto Ulster County 49. Go 1.4 miles. At the fork where there is a road maintenance shed in the center of the triangle called "Millbrook," bear right. Now comes a long drive past beautiful Catskill farms, the circa-1902 covered bridge at Grants Mills, cottages, and woods for 12.3 miles to a T-intersection. Turn left here and drive for 4.7 miles to another T-intersection. Turn left onto Barkaboom Road and drive 6.4 miles to Ulster County 54. At this point you will pass Big Pond (state property) on your left and then Little Pond State Campground on your right in Delaware County, and may decide to go there instead of chasing after Alder Lake. If not, then turn left toward Turnwood. Go for 1.5 miles on Ulster County 54. At this point you cross a bridge over the Beaverkill, and Ulster County 54 hooks sharply left. Continue for 2.3 miles as Ulster County 54 leads past the Beaverkill fish hatchery and follows Alder Creek upstream. The road turns to dirt and seasonal use only. At the fork, bear right along a rough road for 0.3 mile to parking at a chain across the entrance. Do not block the entrance.

From the New York Thruway take exit 16 for NY 17 west for about 50 miles to exit 96 in Livingston Manor. Turn onto Sullivan County 179 north toward Beaverkill, Deckertown, and Lewbeach. In

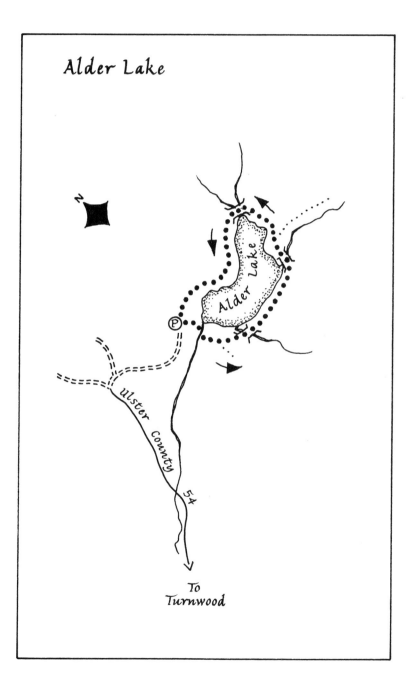

Alder Lake

Alder Lake

Ulster County

54

To
Turnwood

1.2 miles turn right onto Sullivan County 151/Johnson Hill Road toward Beaverkill. Drive for 4.1 miles to Beaverkill, where Sullivan County 151 runs into Sullivan County 152. Continue straight for 4 miles, where you cross into Ulster County and the road becomes Ulster County 54. Continue for 3 miles past the entrance to Little Pond State Campground to Turnwood. Follow directions above from Turnwood.

Trail

Go around the chain at the entrance to the abandoned Coykendall Lodge. This property was originally owned in the 1850s by a farmer named Janis Smith, who farmed rocks more than he did land. He decided the land was useless, dammed Alder Creek, and created a fish hatchery. George Coykendall, general superintendent of Ulster and Delaware Railroad in Kingston, bought Mr. Smith's property and built the lodge you see. In the 1940s he sold the place to a hunting and fishing club. Alder Lake and the Catskills are known for a unique strain of large brook trout that attains lengths up to 16 and 17 inches. Most brook trout are 6 to 10 inches, at the most.

Go down to the lake where the Alder Lake Loop Trail begins, designated by red trail markers. Turn right across the dam. Follow the field edge to your right, away from the water, and take the second old woods road, grass-covered, headed uphill. (The first old road follows Alder Creek downstream.) Keep on this road past an intersection of side trails (vague enough that you might miss them) to a left turn on another old road at the top of the rise. The key to following the red trail around Alder Lake is to follow the trail markers. Sometimes it is a road, other times it is a path.

Toward the head of the lake, cross a bridge over one of the lake's feeder streams. At the fork keep left, always following the red trail around the lake. Watch for old beaver lodges against the shore. There may even be some recent chewing activity. The red trail leaves the old roadbed and heads left along the shore. Out on the water you may hear male green frogs proclaiming their territories with a re-sounding "Gung!"

At the third bridge grows a small meadow of tall meadow rue, cow parsnip, dock, blue iris, and bee-balm. This last *(Monarda didyama)* is also called Oswego tea and bergamot. It is the scarlet—intense red— cousin of the more common, lilac wild bergamot. The square stem tells you it is a mint. Bee-balm is one of those arresting red flowers whose only equal in the wild is cardinal flower. To come across such brilliance shining among summer's vast greenery takes your breath away.

Bee-balm is highly esteemed by gardeners not only for its color but also because it is a principal food of hummingbirds, and attracts them. A stand as large as this can support a pair of hummingbirds. Want to see one? Sit a few yards away in the trail, or stand beside a tree trunk nearby, and wait a few minutes. The flowers must be in bloom and the weather must be pleasant. Remain perfectly motion- less. You will hear the hummingbird before you see it, a sound like a big bug that approaches quickly as a zooming bee. The humming comes from the blur of the wings, which beat at least 75 times a second.

Suddenly a hummingbird is at the bee-balm, humming and darting about, the iridescent body held upright as it gives you the eye, able to hover or move up, down, sideways, and backwards. Be assured it will spot you, but if you remain unobtrusive, quiet, and still, it may dip its long bill into the bee-balm tubes one by one and, in a matter of moments, divest the entire flower head of its nectar. If it is alarmed, as it probably will be by your presence, the hummingbird will chirp a few times, perhaps alight on a branch to look at you, and then careen away at about 40 mph. This entire performance will last mere seconds. The bird will return in about 15 minutes to feed again.

If the hummingbird you saw was green-gray with a white breast, it was a female ruby-throated hummingbird. If it flashed like a green jewel and had a red throat, you saw a male. Sometimes in the shade the red throat will appear black. It is the only species of hummingbird in the eastern United States and Canada. These, the smallest of birds, fly all the way to Alder Lake from their wintering grounds in Florida, Mexico, and Panama. I find it formidable to conceive of these minute creatures making such a journey twice a year for the duration of their lives. Those that cross the Gulf of Mexico—

*Residents of Sullivan and Delaware Counties have the easiest access
to this human-made lake snuggled on the western side of the
Beaverkill Range and Mill Brook Ridge.*

500 miles—do so in a 26-hour, nonstop flight. Hummingbirds live
solely in the Americas. Europeans must have been entranced when
they first encountered them.

Cross a fourth bridge and pass wet woods of ash, ironwood,
shadbush, northern arrowwood *(Viburnum recognitum),* and steeple-
bush spirea. There is very little intrusive purple loosestrife on Alder
Lake. Ironwood *(Carpinus caroliniana)* trunks look like muscled arms.
Getting closer to the dam, you will pass a shrubby field area grown
up in milkweed *(Aesclepias syriaca).* If it is getting on to dusk, the trout
will be rising, disturbing the quiet lake surface with freshening rings.

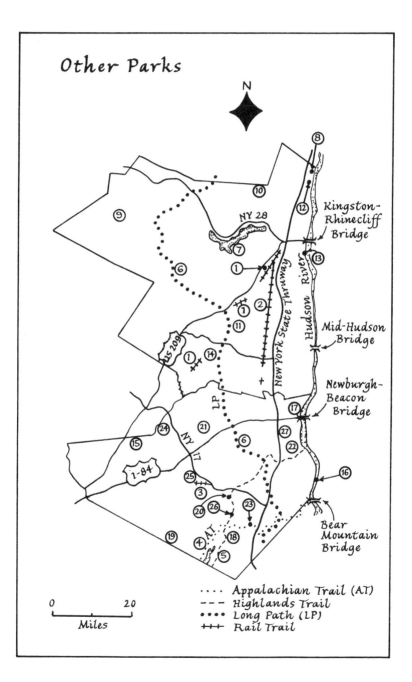

Other Parks

N

NY 28

Kingston-
Rhinecliff
Bridge

Hudson River

New York State Thruway

Mid-Hudson
Bridge

US 209

LP

Newburgh-
Beacon
Bridge

NY 17

I-84

AT

Bear
Mountain
Bridge

9
10
8
12
13
7
6
1
2
1
11
1
14
24
21
15
6
17
27
22
16
25
3
20
26
23
19
4
18
5

0   20
Miles

···· Appalachian Trail (AT)
---- Highlands Trail
•••• Long Path (LP)
+++ Rail Trail

Other Parks to Walk and Ramble Through

Rail Trails

Sections of the former lines of the railroad companies Ontario and Western (O&W), Wallkill Valley, and Delaware and Hudson (D&H) are being converted to trails. These rail trails are built and maintained by volunteers whose organizations seek donations to continue converting former railbeds to trails.

The railbeds are straight, wide, level cinder paths where you can walk, jog, bike, ride horses, ski, or snowshoe. Unlike woodland footpaths, rail trails were once transportation corridors and are often elevated above the immediate surrounding area with no place to sit or rest. Some rail trails provide benches, such as the Wallkill Valley Rail Trail through New Paltz. The rail trails run straight through the bottomland of Ulster and Orange Counties past old farmland, pastureland, marshland, backyards, creeks, and woods. They are a good place to come for the first signs of spring and for fall colors, but in the summertime the cinder bed can be very hot and dry at midday.

1. O&W Rail Trail

This railroad replaced the D&H Canal. Seventeen miles exist from Kingston southwest through Hurley, Rosendale, and Cottekill to Kyserike. Then there is another 3.5-mile section along Rondout Creek from Accord to Kerhonkson; and another 1.25 miles in Ellenville. Plans call to connect these three sections and extend the route to Cuddebackville and Monticello with a spur from Spring Glen to Liberty. For more information, call 914-687-9311.

2. Wallkill Valley Rail Trail

This walk is 12.2 miles from the New Paltz/Rosendale town line to the Gardiner/Shawangunk town line. A half-mile section is in Wallkill south of the correctional facility. Plans call to connect these. For more information, write to the Wallkill Valley Rail Trail Association, PO Box 1048, New Paltz, NY 12561-1048. Another privately owned 3-mile section is open to the public from Rosendale Wallkill trestle bridge to New Paltz. A visit to this section may spark your interest in the cement industry. For more information on Rosendale cement mines and kilns, visit the A.J. Snyder Estate on NY 213; 914-658-9900.

3. Heritage Trail

This trail follows the former Erie railbed, 2.5 miles from Hartley Road in Wawayanda past 6½ Station Road to Goshen. Plans are to extend the trail through Goshen, Chester, and Monroe to Harriman. For more information, call 914-344-8131.

Long-Distance Paths

4. Appalachian Trail

Other than the few places mentioned in the text, you can hike the 2150-mile, white-marked AT by joining it at any point where it crosses a road. Most of these are one-way routes, with return the same way. From the ridge overlooking Greenwood Lake, you can see New York City. From Mombasha High Point in winter there is a 360-degree view, partially through trees, of Schunemunk, the Harriman hills, Mount Peter, and the Ramapos. See "Fitzgerald Falls" and "Little Dam Pond," described below. Of course you can drive as well as walk to the summit of Bear Mountain, but this is the original and first part of the trail to be built in America, so to walk it is fitting. From the summit and tower you gain vast views, from the skyscrapers of New York City to the Catskill peaks. At the zoo the AT drops to its lowest elevation along the entire route, approaching sea level. It is fun to run into the through-hikers on their way to Maine and spend some time chatting with them at a lean-to. Each one has a trail name and many interesting tales. For more information, write to the Appalachian Trail Conference, PO Box 807, Harpers Ferry, WV 25425-0807; 304-535-6331.

5. Highlands Trail

On this trail, you can travel from the Delaware River in New Jersey to the Hudson River at Storm King. It uses existing trails, some of which are covered in this book: Sterling Ridge Trail to Appalachian Trail to Goose Pond State Park to Orange County Rail Trail east of Chester to Schunemunk Mountain to Black Rock Forest to Storm King. For more information, call the New York–New Jersey Trail Conference, 212-685-9699.

6. Long Path

You can follow the turquoise markers of the 214-mile Long Path anywhere you see them cross a road. Legally parking your car can be a problem, however. The path extends from the George Washington Bridge in New York City through both Orange and Ulster Counties to the northern Catskills. Some sections are closed while legal questions of access over private property are resolved. Call the New York–New Jersey Trail Conference at 212-685-9699 before you go.

Ulster County

7. Ashokan Reservoir

Visitors to the Catskills often feel the mountains lack a visible sense of history. There are few old buildings and historic sites that predate the grand-hotel era. The fault lies largely in this reservoir, which dammed the Esopus River for New York City's drinking-water supply. It flooded the well-settled heartland of the Catskills, forcing the relocation of seven towns and 2000 inhabitants.

The pedestrian walkway along the dam is a popular stroll with fabulous views of Ashokan High Point. On NY 28 in Shokan at Winchell's Corner, turn onto New York City Road toward Olive Bridge. Follow this for 1.9 miles. Cross the reservoir on a causeway. At the stop sign, turn left onto Monument Road. In 0.1 mile, where the road goes downhill (actually down-dam), park at the upper-level gate beside the road. Good birding during spring and fall migration.

8. Bristol Beach State Park

This Hudson River site may become developed as a boat launch. For now, lawns at various heights overlooking and on the water give nice river views. The tidal cove is a good birding site, but access is by bushwhacking only. It is located north of Saugerties on Eavesport Road.

9. Catskill Mountain Trailheads

Anywhere within the Blue Line—the forever-wild state lands of the Catskills—that you see a trailhead, you can park and go for a stroll. Most trailheads parallel clear mountain brooks through enchanting forests, sometimes even for miles, before any serious climbing of peaks. Some notable trailheads:

1. On the south side of Balsam Lake Mountain; parking at Quaker Clearing trailhead with a walk along the Beaver Kill.
2. Just south of Big Indian; parking at the end of Lost Clove Road with a path along Lost Clove Brook.
3. From Oliverea, parking at the end of McKenley Hollow with a walk into the slope of Balsam Mountain.
4. Park at the end of Denning Road, past Frost Valley YMCA, and walk the woods along the Neversink.

Two other exceptional mountains for long hikes are Panther (from Shandaken) and Table Mountain/Peekamoose Mountain. You can also hike the ski trails of Belleayre in the warm season.

10. Magic Meadow

This truly magical place, especially at dawn or the firefly-lit dusk, is owned by the Woodstock Guild. Follow directions to Overlook Mountain, but continue past that trailhead about half a mile downhill to a pull-off on your right. A short trail under hemlocks leads across a brook and into the meadow.

11. Mohonk Mountain House

This resort, founded in 1869, preserves the genteel tradition of the European-style hotel in the mountains. The many groomed trails and carriageways were designed for aesthetic appreciation. My favorite route to Sky Top is through the Labyrinth to the Crevice. One of the best 360-degree views in the region is from Sky Top. You can see almost all of the sites described in this book. A day pass, with map, is available to hikers. This entitles you to use of the grounds, carriage

The Rondout Lighthouse opposite Sleightsburg Spit

roads, trails, lawns, flower garden, and barn museum. Hikers may not enter the hotel or use swimming facilities. No dogs are allowed. Fees are $6 midweek, $9 weekends and holidays for adults; for children under 12, $4 midweek, $5 weekends and holidays; for families with children under 12, $16 midweek, $23 weekends and holidays. Parking for hikers is only allowed at the gatehouse, which is nearly 3 miles downhill from Sky Top. A shuttle to the picnic lodge runs daily June 1 through Labor Day and often on weekends the rest of the year. It costs $2 per person round trip. For information, call 914-255-1000.

12. Seaman Park

Located just north of Saugerties along US 9W, this town park is good for a stroll with small children who are just beginning to explore nature. There are flower gardens, fountains, lawn, an old road along the woods' edge, deciduous and coniferous trees, picnic tables, and swings. Terwilliger's gristmill, built in 1750, is under restoration.

13. Sleightsburg Spit

Scenic Hudson is turning over this 30-acre historic site to the Town of Esopus, which will in the future open the park to visitors. It is located on the south bank of the mouth of the Rondout Creek between Kingston and Port Ewen. This was the terminus of the D&H

Canal. Photographs from the shipping era show monstrous cranes, mountains of Pennsylvania coal, and fleets of barges. All that is left are sunken barges, rotting pier timbers, and scattered dregs of anthracite. An old woods road currently leads out (almost) to tidal coves and mud flats with great views of Rondout Lighthouse and the Hudson River.

14. Smiley Road, Sam's Point, and Napanoch Point

The natural communities of the northern Shawangunk are unique and beautiful. Sam's Point is the highest in the range. It lies within a 4000-acre plateau tract owned as watershed lands by the Town of Ellenville. Here are the bulk of the globally unique ridgetop dwarf pitch pines, the larger ice caves, and High Point. Twenty-five years ago Ellenville granted a 50-year lease for this land to a tourist attraction called Ice Caves Mountain. For $6 per adult, $4 per child, you can drive to Sam's Point and visit the nearby, smaller ice caves, but there is no legal access to the rest of the parcel with its unmaintained trails except along Smiley Road.

Smiley Road carriageway once connected Ellenville to Lake Minnewaska. So long as you see the New York–New Jersey Trail Conference blazes on this old road, you know you have legal access to Napanoch Point. You can walk in either from Lake Awosting in Lake Minnewaska State Park (a very long hike), or from the other end that begins behind the firehouse in Ellenville (where parking is a problem). Use trail map 9 from the Trail Conference, available in bookstores. Watch for future changes in access.

Orange County

15. Bashakill Wildlife Management Area

Two thousand one hundred seventy-five acres of marsh, swamp, and forest protect enormous numbers of waterfowl, amphibians, reptiles, and who knows what else. Only the tip of this state property lies in Orange County, but it is the all-important parking lot that gives trailhead access to a rail trail in Sullivan County. From Cuddebackville proceed north on US 209 for 3 miles to a right on Otisville Road. (Note the D&H Canal snubbing post in one private front yard.) Turn left onto Indian Orchard Road. Parking is on your left. The railroad embankment extends for miles along the edge of the wetland.

16. Constitution Island

Although located in Putnam County, access to this US Army site is from South Dock at West Point. The Constitution Island Association runs guided tours from mid-June to the last week in September, Wednesday and Thursday, at 1 and 2 PM (times may vary). The island is used by West Point cadets for picnicking. The public is restricted to a tour of historic Warner House and the nearby Revolutionary War redoubt and battery foundations. Throughout the boat ride and walking tour are some of the finest views of World's End and the Hudson Highlands. Reservations are required; call 914-446-8676.

17. Cronomer Hill Park

Located 3 miles north of Newburgh on NY 300, this nearly 60 acre, county-owned park was known in the past for its unsurpassable Hudson River views. The park was closed due to vandalism and lack of funds, yet is open to walkers. Park at the locked gate. For information, call 914-457-3111.

18. Fitzgerald Falls

A 25-foot sliding cascade tumbles within a hemlock forest on the Appalachian Trail. From Greenwood Lake village, take Orange County 5 north for 3 miles to the trail's crossing. Be sure to park on trail land only. Go east on the white-marked Appalachian Trail. Cross beneath a high-tension power line. It is a short walk along the marked trail to the foot of the falls, best in spring and early summer. If you continue, the trail climbs alongside the falls and along a gorgeous mountain hemlock ravine.

19. Frankel Sanctuary

On Blooms Corners Road in Warwick, owned by Orange Audubon Society, this preserved cattail wetland is a good place to pull off on the side of the road at the overlook and watch the birdlife.

20. Goose Pond State Park

This 1600-acre, undeveloped tract of land between Chester and Monroe contains horseback riding trails sometimes abused by off-road vehicles. Lazy Hill Road, a former town road, travels through the park. The entrance is on Lazy Hill Road, but you cannot park here. There is legal, unmarked parking across the street on the corner of Oxford Road/Orange County 51 and NY 17M.

21. Highland Lakes State Park

Popular with horseback riders and illegal off-road vehicles, this 3000-acre state property in the town of Wallkill is crisscrossed by numerous unmarked trails, old marked trails, and abandoned dirt roads. It is a great place to explore, but there are a number of entrances blocked by gates where parking is a problem. The best parking is at Camp Orange and Prospect Roads. The park is a good place for fall walking, since no hunting is allowed, although poaching does occur. Unfortunately, many ticks have been reported here.

22. Kenridge Farm

Museum of the Hudson Highlands

There are 200 acres here, about half of which are hayfields and the other half woods and wetland. Old logging roads run throughout. It is on US 9W in Cornwall, at the foot of Black Rock. For information, call 914-534-7781.

23. Little Dam Lake

A lovely lake along the Appalachian Trail makes a fine destination for a short hike of about 1 mile round trip, with entrance and return along the same route. The lake supports the largest cricket frog population in Orange County. You can hear choruses of these tiny frogs in June. Access is from Orange County 19 just north of Tuxedo.

24. Moonbeams Wildlife Sanctuary

This Nature Conservancy property of 150 acres may be changing ownership. Unmarked paths through fields and forest explore an abandoned dairy farm. The most interesting feature is the Shawangunk

Kill, which forms the parcel's western boundary. No dogs are allowed. The sanctuary is open dawn to dusk. From Middletown, go north on NY 17 to exit 118 at Fair Oaks. Turn north on Ulster County 76. Go 1.4 miles to a left on Prosperous Valley Road (the road on your right is Shawangunk Road). Proceed 2.3 miles to roadside parking on your left. The house here is private (belonging to the Moons, who gifted the farm to the Conservancy), but the property on both sides of the road belongs to the preserve. Trails begin opposite the house at the preserve sign and on the same side as the house at the far north corner of their private property.

25. 6½ Station Road Wildlife Sanctuary

Owned by the Orange County Audubon Society, this excellent birding spot in Goshen is named for a spot nearby where the Erie Railroad crossed. Here was a pickup station for farmers' milk cans 6½ miles from the creamery. The site is mostly marshland, with a short overlook trail. From Goshen take West Church Street beneath the Quickway onto NY 17M. At the stoplight, turn right onto 6½ Station Road. The sanctuary comes in about a mile on your right. Watch for an open field downhill with a view of a marsh. The sanctuary sign at the parking area faces the road and is hard to see.

26. Sterling Forest

This is 17,500 acres of privately owned wilderness, in the Tuxedo Mountains between Harriman State Park and New Jersey, famous for its historic iron mines, rocky ridges, clear waters, and unspoiled second-growth forest. It is currently owned by overseas investors with high hopes of developing it into a city. Citizen and government groups are working to preserve the place. Watch for further developments. Should you wish to help with those developments, contact Sterling Forest Resources, 914-294-3098. Hiker access is now restricted and may become denied. Currently, only two trails are open to hikers during the daytime and only during March, April, June, July, and August (not May): the 8.4-mile Sterling Ridge and the 2-mile Allis Trails, both blazed in blue. Sterling Ridge Trail can be followed all the way to New Jersey at Hewitt. On the Greenwood Lake end are the ruins of another "Baron" Hasenclever iron mine. Atop the ridge stands the newly refurbished fire tower, with a spectacular 360-degree view. Parking is on a pull-off on the south side of NY 17A between Greenwood Lake and Tuxedo. Allis Trail connects Sterling Ridge Trail to the Appalachian Trail at Fitzgerald Falls. A free day-use permit is required from the owners, Sterling Forest Corporation, located on Orange County 84/Sterling Lake Road. For information, call 914-351-2356.

27. New Windsor Cantonment

If you find yourself just north of Vails Gate on NY 300 yearning to stretch your legs, stop in at this state historic site. Stroll the lawn past log cabins and camps of this important Revolutionary War site. George Washington quartered the American army—7000 troops—here for over a year trying to wrap up the Revolution. Open mid-April through October, Wednesday through Saturday 10 AM–5 PM, Sunday 1–5 PM; also open Memorial Day, Independence Day, and Labor Day. For information, call 914-561-1765.

Hudson River Bridges

These are wonderful places to observe the awesome current of the Hudson River ripping past channel buoys. You will see grand colors in autumn, ice floes in winter. The bridges are an excellent alternative if you cannot climb mountains; the spaciousness feels similar.

Bear Mountain Bridge

Walkways pass along both sides of the bridge. There are invigorating, high and windy, large views. Upriver past Con Hook and the cone of Sugarloaf is West Point. Downriver are Iona Island, The Timp, and the South Gate of the Hudson Highlands between Dunderberg and Manitou Mountains. Bear Mountain and Popolopen Gorge and Torne are west, Anthony's Nose east. Ten-minute parking is available on the west bank beside the tollbooths at a public phone, and on the east bank just north of the bridge on a pull-off along NY 9D. Or, you can park for a fee at the Bear Mountain Inn, and stroll past Hessian Lake, the Trailside Museum, monuments, and views to the bridge.

Mid-Hudson Bridge

Great views are found along the pedestrian walkway. Follow directions given below to the Poughkeepsie-Highland railroad bridge, but continue on Haviland Road to its end at Johnson-Iorio Memorial Park for parking. This bridge is not for those afraid of heights. You will find windy views of Poughkeepsie and Kaal Rock, upriver to the railroad bridge and Crum Elbow, downriver to the Beacon Range in clear weather. Open dawn to dusk.

Newburgh-Beacon Bridge

Park on town roads on the Newburgh end and walk up to the pedestrian walkway. Do not park on the Dutchess County side. Best views of Newburgh Bay and the North Gate of the Hudson Highlands are here.

Walkway Over the Hudson

Poughkeepsie-Highland Railroad Bridge Company, Inc.

Plans call for planking this old train trestle, but for now the fearless can walk out to the first American flag staked halfway between the west bank and the river's central channel. Views north are of Crum Elbow, east are to the city of Poughkeepsie and the Fishkill Range, and south are along the Long Reach to the Beacon Range. The trestle is higher than the neighboring Mid-Hudson Bridge. Guided tours are available; call for information on dates and hours. Open all year. Don't even dream of bringing your dog. From intersection of US 9W and US 44/NY 55, go north on US 9W a few hundred yards to the first traffic light. Turn left on Haviland Road (small state sign here for bridge pedestrians and bike route). The entrance is in 0.5 mile on your left beside an electric switching station. Parking is on the left side of the road. For information, call 914-454-9649.

Selected Bibliography

Appalachian Mountain Club. *In the Hudson Highlands*. Walking News, Inc., 1945. Older collection of stories on history and folklore.

Beers, F.W. *Atlas of Orange County* and *Atlas of Ulster County*. Beers, Ellis, and Soule, 1867. Available at historical societies. Good for looking at old roads and location of settlements.

Boyle, Robert H. *The Hudson River, A Natural and Unnatural History*, expanded edition. W.W. Norton, 1979. Details on the story of Storm King and Consolidated Edison, plus much more.

Evers, Alf. *The Catskills from Wilderness to Woodstock*. Overlook Press, 1982, reprint of 1972 original. The classic. A complete history of the Catskills.

Gilcrest, Ann. *Footsteps Across Cement, A History of the Township of Rosendale, New York*. 1976. Available on loan at Rosendale Library. Thorough explanation of the local tanning, cement, and D&H Canal industries.

Glunt, Ruth R. *Lighthouses and Legends of the Hudson*. Library Research Associates, 1975. A classic.

Howell, William Thompson. *The Hudson Highlands*. Walking News, Inc., 1982, reprint of the 1933–34 original. Stories, descriptions, and photographs from the turn of the century. Another classic.

Kick, Peter, Barbara McMartin, and James McMartin Long. *50 Hikes in the Hudson Valley*, 2nd edition. Backcountry Publications, 1994. Selected hikes.

Kiviat, Erik. *The Northern Shawangunks, An Ecological Survey*. Mohonk Preserve, Inc., 1988. Best description of Shawangunk ecology.

McAllister, Lee and Myron Steven Ochman. *Hiking the Catskills*. New York–New Jersey Trail Conference, 1989. All-inclusive guide to the Catskills.

McIntosh, Robert P. *The Forests of the Catskill Mountains, New York*. Hope Farm Press, 1977. Scientific paper.

Myles, William J. *Harriman Trails, A Guide and History*. New York–New Jersey Trail Conference, 1991. All-inclusive guide to trails and history.

New York–New Jersey Trail Conference. *New York Walk Book*, 5th edition. Anchor Books/Doubleday, 1984. Good overview guide.

O'Brien, Raymond J. *American Sublime, Landscape and Scenery of the Lower Hudson Valley*. Columbia University Press, 1981. History of the value and movement of aesthetics and landscape.

Snyder, Bradley. *The Shawangunk Mountains, A History of Nature and Man*. Mohonk Preserve, Inc., 1981. Good overview.

Titus, Robert. *The Catskills, A Geological Guide*. Purple Mountain Press, 1993.

Van Loan. *Catskill Mountain Guide*. Hope Farm Press, reprint of the 1879 original. Fun to read the hotel advertisements.

Van Zandt, Roland. *Chronicles of the Hudson, Three Centuries of Travelers' Accounts*. Rutgers University Press, 1971.

Wyckoff, Jerome. *Rock Scenery of the Hudson Highlands and Palisades*. Adirondack Mountain Club, 1971. Excellent field guide.